MARRIAGE GEMS

Deji Ajayi

BOOKBUILDERS • EDITIONS AFRICA

ISBN: 978-978-921-247-7

Published in Nigeria by
BookBuilders • Editions Africa
2 Awosika Avenue, Bodija, Ibadan
email: folatundeus@yahoo.com
mobile: 08068052154

Printed in Ibadan
Oluben Printers, Oke-Ado
mobile: 0805 522 0209

Cover design
Tunde Omirin
08128882628

Dedication

This book is dedicated to our God, the giver of life and the one who orders our steps in life! And to my father, Chief Alex Olu Ajayi, Odoba Ahusi of Ado Ekiti, as well as my four mothers: Mama Marian Ademubiola Ajayi, my grandmother, Mama Ajike Ibironke Oluwa (nee Adekunle), my first mum, Mama Adeline Olufunmilayo Ajayi (nee Adeyemi), my big mummy, and Mama Adedoyin Olufunmilayo (nee Oduyemi), my youngest mum. You all taught me the essence of living a dutiful and God-fearing life. Your tutelage has been my mainstay till this day.

To my darling wife, Aderinola and our children, Oludare, Ayomide and Ayokunmi, as well as 'Tomilayo, thanks for proving yourselves steadfast both in season and out of season.

To my ever loving band of brothers, sisters and cousins, that continue to spur me on to be consistent as an enigma in our extended family.

Contents

Foreword

In the sacred institution of marriage, we find a beautiful tapestry woven with threads of love, commitment, sacrifice, and faith. It is a divine union ordained by God Himself, designed to reflect His unconditional love for us. Yet, in the midst of life's challenges and complexities, maintaining harmony and peace within the marriage bond can sometimes feel like an uphill battle.

In his insightful book, *Marriage Gems*, Deji Ajayi offers a treasure trove of practical wisdom and invaluable advice for couples seeking to navigate the journey of marriage with grace and wisdom. Drawing from his own and shared experiences, as well as timeless biblical principles, Deji provides a roadmap for cultivating deeper intimacy, fostering open communication, and resolving conflicts in a spirit of humility and love.

As I reflect on the pages of this book, I am reminded of the words of King Solomon, the wisest man who ever lived, as recorded in the book of Proverbs: "Two are better than one because they have a good reward for their labour. For if they fall, one will lift up his companion. But woe to him who is alone when he falls, for he has no one to help him up. Again, if two lie down together, they will keep warm; but how can one be warm alone? Though one may be overpowered by another, two can withstand him. And a threefold cord is not quickly broken" (Ecclesiastes 4:9-12).

In these verses, we find a profound truth about the power and strength that comes from the union of two individuals in marriage. It is a partnership forged not only in love but also in mutual support, encouragement and companionship. And when God is invited into the centre of that union, as the third cord binding husband and wife together, the bond becomes unbreakable.

Deji's book serves as a timely reminder of the importance of building our marriages on the solid foundation of faith in God and His Word. Through practical tips, insightful anecdotes, and heartfelt encouragement, he equips couples with the tools they need to nurture and strengthen their relationship, even in the face of adversity.

To the author, Deji, I commend you for your courage and transparency in sharing your journey and insights with us. Your passion for strengthening marriages and honouring God through your own relationship is evident on every page. May your words inspire and encourage countless couples to pursue deeper levels of intimacy, communication and unity in their marriages.

To the readers, I urge you to approach this book with open hearts and minds, ready to glean wisdom and guidance for your own marriage journey. Whether you are newlyweds embarking on the adventure of a lifetime or seasoned couples seeking to reignite the flame of love and passion, there is something within these pages for you.

May *Marriage Gems* be a beacon of hope and encouragement for all who turn its pages, guiding them toward greater love, joy and fulfillment in their marriages. And may God's grace and peace abound in your homes as you seek to honour Him in your union.

With blessings and prayers for every marriage represented within these words,

Ven (Dr.) Adeyemi Agbelusi
Lagos 2024

Preface: A Word from the Author

To derive joy in life, you need to make yourself and people around you happy. A greater percentage of this joy if quantified, stems out of success of one's marriage. Our last book, *Management Gems*, centred on guiding employees to have a successful career. However, you may not have a successful career if you do not have a successful married life. Thus, we arrive at the birthing of *Marital Gems*, which is a compendium of contemporary ways of leading an impactful and spirit filled marital life.

There are insurmountable issues and topics under marriage and this can neither be exhausted in a book as this, nor in a life time. Reason being that couples are created differently and they have to learn to complement each other and serve as help meet to each other.

In this regard, we have a section "Counsellors Speak" for professionals to share their experience and views on some topics which address other day to day issues in marriage, which might have been left out or not treated in-depth, but desired under the main topics of this book. A number of real life examples were given to buttress some of the topics; where they resemble some of your life experiences, we believe that you will accept them as coincidences, occurrences and happenstance in human lives.

The spiritual aspect of marital life is emphasized, as over the years, we get to understand that the physical life is driven by the spiritual. This informed our quoting tremendously from the Holy Bible. Some of these quotes are familiar and they serve as a refresher for open minds. We hope and pray that this book impacts society positively and encourages other willing writers on marriage to give back their best to society.

Deji Ajayi

Acknowledgements

Joy fills my heart as I have the grace to write the acknowledgement to this work. It is a great pleasure to acknowledge the support and inspiration of my Wife, Olori Aderinola Taiwo Ajayi, during the course of writing this Book. I cannot but mention the commitment of Venerable (Dr) Paul Adeyemi Agbelusi in accepting to pen the Foreword to this Book; which I refer to as "the exhortation of Paul." You have always been my Spiritual mentor over the years. To my Professional mentor, Elder Johnson Oluwasuji, I say a big thank you. Kudos to the renowned Marriage Counsellor, Mrs Dupe Ehirim. I appreciate all your contributions to this Book, especially under the Chapter, "Counsellors Speak." I trust that present and future generations will gain a great deal from your admonition.

Those early morning meet up at Sweet Sensation, Ogba, Lagos, to review my typed manuscript with Sister Funmi Abiloye are highly appreciated. I am most grateful for your consistency, which gave this Book its fulcrum. I will always cherish my Sister, Bisade Ogunlade, for fishing you out! I cannot but gloriously felicitate with my Brother, 'Tilewa Oluwa "Gboogboo Associates!" for making power available heedlessly during the course of writing this Book.

To my dearest friends, at home and in the Diaspora, too numerous to mention, who gave this book the desired push, so it sees the light of the day. I doff my Hat for your commitment and loyalty to our lifelong friendship. One of the best encouraging statements made by them was: "Thank you too, Deji, for sharing your knowledge and experience with the world in the form of Books. Well done!" God will continue to bless your marriages in the glorious years ahead. Amen.

ACKNOWLEDGEMENTS

To my Publisher, Akintunde Akinola, thanks for accommodating all my requests, wishing you continuous successes in your future endeavours.

Deji Ajayi
March, 2024

"FROLICKING SINGLES"

"But life is worth nothing unless I use it for doing the work assigned to me by the Lord Jesus – the work of telling others the Good News about God's mighty kindness and love" Acts 20:24 (TLB)

Relishing bachelorhood and spinsterhood can be very interesting in our part of the world. Having been released from the four walls of the university to the National Service year, we experience a great deal of freedom. While the bachelors see a long period of "waiting" to pick a spouse, the spinsters believe they have a short period to relax or wait. So, while the bachelors throw caution to the wind in their new found freedom, the spinsters tread with caution. Engaging in unending partying, with the heralding of every weekend is the call of the bachelors, who are ready to travel from one end of town to the other, or from one state to the other to catch the fun desired.

Shuttling between Abuja and Kaduna by road for many Youth Corp members was child's play as part of the frolick of their bachelor years, having just been exposed to funds being paid by government as stipend for the service year, which was presumably higher than the income or allowances received from parents while in college. Lagos to Ibadan axis was another area for parties, which provided an opportunity to visit old friends and showcase lost fads and crazes.

In as much as singles should seek fun on leaving college, everything must be done in moderation. In our days, we had cases of friends drinking to stupor and on getting home, being unable to open their gates, ending up sleeping in their cars overnight. In another case, a friend slept at his gate and was beaten by heavy rain, but only woke up in the morning after the rain had subsided. We also had cases of people losing their lives through accidents while driving home from parties and, as a result of excess wine, could not control their speed.

1

The ability to utilize the freedom of bachelorhood and spinsterhood to carry out self-development should be the driving force. It is an opportunity to specialize. In our days, we had friends who made use of the service year to commence their professional examinations in their various institutes, such as the Institute of Chartered Accountants of Nigeria (ICAN), the Institute of Personal Management of Nigeria (CIPMN), the Nigerian Institute of Management (NIM), the Nigerian Institute of Marketing (NIMARK), the Nigerian Institute of Purchasing and Supply (NIPS) and others. These preparation and qualifications put many in the right stead for quality employment immediately after the National Service. A number of these were in the multinational companies within Nigeria.

Employment threw many singles across the country to far-flung places. We had people who grew up in Lagos in the southwest gaining employment in Calabar, in the south-south region of the country. Also, many bachelors and spinsters moved from all parts of the country to Lagos and Port Harcourt, being major industrial cities, for employment. Finding oneself in a new environment elicits opportunities of building new relationships and ideas. It was necessary to bond with the reality of the diversity one finds himself or herself.

In some other cases, some singles reached out and formed or joined branches of their secondary school associations — Old Students Associations — thus taking up responsibilities in the social aspect of life. Not too long, some became General Secretaries, Presidents, Chairmen, etc, of the associations. I was the General Secretary of my set for one of my old secondary schools — Christ's School, Ado-Ekiti — in the Lagos Branch. It was a privilege to be saddled with great responsibility at an early age, organizing members with diverse ideas, and bringing them to see the need to bond and work for the upliftment of our alma mater.

Being in employment as a single is also a platform to reveal opportunities to other friends searching for jobs, as you are able to see vacancies available in your organization, as well as in organizations of other friends who are already gainfully employed. In my own instance, I was privileged to work with the Director of Administration of NBC, Chief Tawose, and his office was responsible for the recruitment of managers into the company at entry, middle and senior levels. I seized this opportunity to inform friends of vacancies existing so that they could apply. A number of them eventually were employed through this simple information. My Boss always joked, saying: "you have added your friends to the list, Deji," referring to the shortlist of candidates for aptitude tests during selection process. Surely, he knew I will only shortlist qualified friends!!

Having secured employment, friends began to seek stable relationships which was very much in order, as it is pertinent to state that some continued with their university or national service relationships. These stable old relationships triggered many other singles to get serious as it also sent right signals to them as being able to achieve such feat, only if they were focused. It was a charge to the singles to be more spiritual, asking God for "the bone of my bone and the flesh of my flesh," while those who were "hooked", referring to those with stable relationships, moved on to the next level of getting adequate accommodation to start a new life and get to know members of each other's families, as well as build stronger relationships. Having been "hooked" with my current wife as my fiancé, I endeavoured to intimate myself with members of her family. I traveled from time to time to visit and attend their family functions, and also invited her to mine when the occasion arose.

At this stage, bachelors and spinsters get a great deal of push back from friends and relatives, asking so many questions. A few of the questions I can remember are: "Hope you have certified your blood groups?," "How well do you know her, as you know women can change with time?" and "Does she work in the bank?" The most frustrating question I got was: "Why don't you find someone about your height?" Such people who asked this question got the right response from me with great equanimity, by letting them know that we were divinely privileged to be giants in my family and that I had also studied my fiancé in terms of morals and I would love to live my life with such a person. This put paid to this question forever!!

With friends choosing dates and receiving conjugal blessings, as well as some of us having the opportunity to attend these occasions, it dawned on many of us to give marriage a pride of place in our list of priorities going forward.

In as much as freedom permeates bachelorhood, we should take into cognizance that this freedom is a delicate one and that it does not last. The good thing for some of us then was that we had senior friends and would be mentors, who urged us on by giving us their own experience in marriage and assured us that "there was no ideal situation in marriage." Some others made fun of us, saying: "You guys want to be men about town? Go and marry!" All these encouraging words made many of us go the whole hog with the confidence that getting married deserved. So, intending couples and singles should endeavour to have senior friends, mentors and experienced married adults that they can learn from by watching them from afar and sharing from their fountain of knowledge and experience.

HOLDING THE HORN OF THE WEDDING - GETTING PREPARED
"The first bond of Society is Marriage"

Marcus Tullius Cicero

As long as you receive the full support of your own family as a bachelor, you will exude the confidence to prepare for marriage. This can only materialize if you have laid all the cards on the table by informing members of your family about your plans to get married, warming your fiancé up to them by introducing her to every required relative at every available occasion. As a spinster, you need to avoid surprises by informing your relatives of your fiance's background, including what he does for a living, which is germane. You should not take things for granted, believing that "anything goes!" No parent will want his daughter to marry someone who does not have a stable source of income, or who is "hustling abroad". You do not expose yourself to danger as a result of desperation. If he is gainfully employed before marriage and later loses his job, which is part of the challenges of marriage. He will surely pick up, but not for you to present an applicant as a future husband! You need to settle that bit so each person moves on in order to maintain joy in their families.

I had to take my fiancé to visit my grandmother in Ado-Ekiti, in southwest Nigeria, a four-hour drive from Lagos. On our way back, we had a stop over to visit one of my aunties in Ibadan. This was after intimating her with my parents, numerous brothers, sisters and friends, as well as cousins. Conviviality gave me the support and confidence needed to prepare adequately for my wedding. By the time I was invited by my fiance's parents for a chat, I was ready for a no holds barred discussion!

Intending couples should take advantage of the counseling sessions, which are mandatory in churches, to serve as a springboard for a successful marriage. Some of the topics taught include, among others: managing finances, intimacy with in-laws, Christian living and raising godly children. You have to insert this in your busy schedule for your preparation to gather momentum. For example, I married from the Catholic Church, and the counseling sessions took twelve weeks! The sessions took place every Friday, modules running from 6pm to 7pm, with my fiancé and I attending alongside other intending couples at St. Leo's Catholic Church, Toyin Street, Ikeja, Lagos. We were given two attendance cards, containing the modules, and were marked and signed on completion of every module. There was a final sign off by the Monsignor at the end of the whole twelve-week counseling session. The sessions were interesting, with true life examples being shared by the various counselors and we all had the opportunity to ask questions on confounding issues.

As the saying goes: "when you anchor your marriage spiritually, no physical force can move you." When dates are picked for wedding by designated priests in Churches, they are ordained, so intending couples should just pray along. They should not subject themselves or give in to the fear being entertained by family members. You may decide to have prayer sessions at the family level, fasting days, vigils, and praise sessions in spiritual preparation for the wedding day. With all these in place, you do not have anything to fear, nor to hide information from some relatives; you will have the guts to speak freely about your wedding. This confidence and faith will dovetail into how you handle your marriage in future. In this wise, friends and relatives need to be involved in planning for the wedding, ranging from purchase of dresses to foodstuff, engagement requirements and all other things. As the intending groom, you cannot do everything, likewise the intending bride hardly should be seen too much on the streets. She is rarely to be seen because she is a jewel which is to be hidden.

ENGAGEMENT /WEDDING DAY

For the couple, the engagement day, which is taken as the 'Traditional Wedding" in this part of the world, as well as the wedding day, is supposed to be a day of joy. They have to relax and smile as much as possible, because they are the cynosure of all eyes. If you frown because you are dissatisfied with a simple occurrence, such as the Master of Ceremonies' activities, or the caterer's inexperience, this posture will be picked unknowingly by the cameraman who is trying to do his job, covering every aspect of the events. In later days and years, when you now want to review or watch the video or check through the photo gallery, you will be surprised to find that you frowned in most of the poses! Alas, this cannot be corrected. So the couple should try as much as possible to be calm at every event about their wedding ceremonies. I remember one of the wedding receptions I attended, the wedding cake could not be delivered until the last part of the programme, because the baker was stuck in a horrible traffic gridlock on Lagos roads that fateful Saturday. However, the groom was smiling throughout the event as if nothing was wrong. The Master of Ceremonies changed the order of events at the reception. Everywhere was serene without any tension. By the time the beautiful wedding cake "the cathedral" was rolled in on a trolley, everyone clapped and the atmosphere was charged with great excitement with the couple's dance!!!

What we are saying in essence is that intending couples should look forward to a successful marriage, not putting so much energy and fuss on the wedding day. Even though we expect a hitch free event, we should take things in their stride and avoid acrimony. Vendors and their team should be warned to maintain peace with everyone they need to interact or work with.

MATCH-MAKING – UPSIDES AND DOWNSIDES

Every man's life is a fairy-tale written by God's fingers

Hans Christian Andersen

Of course matchmaking has its up and down sides in marriage. The match maker is supposed to be humble and thank God that he or she was part of the success of the courtship leading to marriage!! As part of the upsides of matchmaking, the couple will always appreciate and seek the progress of the matchmaker, being available to support him or her when the need arises, morally, financially and psychologically. On the other hand, when the matchmaker tends to be pompous and seen to draw attention to himself or herself, the couple tend to avoid this person, by leaving him out of their events. This is because the couple will see the match maker as focusing on self aggrandizement rather than the success of the marriage.

There is a proverb among the Yoruba of Nigeria in West Africa that says, "Ti iyawo ba m'oju oko tan, alarina a ye ba," which translates to "the matchmaker steps aside when the wife's intimacy with the husband is consolidated." We have cases of the matchmaker trying to lord things over her friend, the wife, and still showing heavy presence in the new couple's home, interfering in personal matters and expecting to be given a pride of place in their home always. There was an instance whereby a matchmaker visited the newly-wed and told the wife that: "I introduced you to 'Mr. B' so that you can enjoy, but you have failed to recognize me by sending some of this largesse my way or that of my family." This was a rude shock to the wife and she prayed her way out of this "enslavement".

It is suggested that as a match maker, you keep your distance after marriage and watch the relationship mature exponentially. You will be much respected with this stance, as the Bible tells us in I Peter 5:5: "Be clothed with humility for God resists the proud, but gives grace to the humble."

SUPPORT REQUIRED FROM IN-LAWS

"Oh my son's my son till he gets him a wife, but my daughter is my daughter all her life."

Dinah Maria Mullock Craik

A great deal of support is expected from in-laws by the newly-wedded couple. For instance, the wife will expect the parents of her husband to guide her regularly having been accepted fully into their family. She will expect to be corrected discreetly every time she makes a mistake. She will not expect to be gossiped by her husband's sisters, rather she will expect camaraderie. Our advice is that where the wife does not get this intimacy, she should accept the husband's siblings as they are and treat them as they deserve.

On the other hand, the new husband believes he should be trusted to take care of his wife who has been handed over to him wholeheartedly. So he expects his parents in-law to treat him automatically as their son and as part of the family, and not as a stranger. He expects to be invited to family ceremonies and events even at short notice, thus enhancing recognition.

Families with strong traditions of elaborate celebrations of birthdays, Christmas, wedding and graduation ceremonies should endeavour to induct the latest member of the family gradually, rather than leaving them behind, because they find it difficult to cope with the pace of events!!

It is a belief in some quarters that newly-weds should not allow relatives in their homes in the first couple of years. We feel circumstances differ. Things will always sort themselves out. We are Africans and we surely have the culture of being our brother's keeper. For instance, if the wife puts to bed, it is customary for the husband's mother or the wife's mother or aunty to come around to support the new mother. Couples should be able to manage the situation of excesses from these relatives. This is part of learning the peculiarities of marriage.

By the time couples start avoiding in-laws or setting formal rules of visits, they will be building an unhealthy wall in their relationships. In my instance, two of my brothers were staying with me before I got married. They had cordial relationships with my wife during our courtship. As they had their own jobs and were also planning to set out in life, the onus was on me to still accommodate them till they were safe and had decent places to move to. This they did within one year of my marriage without any deadline nor friction. Meanwhile, during their stay, these brothers offered to drive my wife to the clinic for her ante-natal appointments. Also, on an occasion, when my wife had bleeding challenges after delivering, one of my brothers who had secured accommodation around my residence was on hand with other loyal friends to take my wife back to the hospital for admission. So, we realize that circumstances differ. We should just allow things to work out as situations permit, leaving God to control the affairs going forward.

This also brings us to the issue of assistance to be given and received from in-laws. In certain circumstances, siblings of either the husband or wife will require some financial support either for education or business. This should be discussed and agreed without any manipulative tendencies. Bills should be presented and visits made to business sites for transparency sake. This gives credence to what Ruth said in the Bible: "...thy people will be my people and thy God my God" (Ruth 1:16b).

Also, as the marriage deepens in years, the couple may require the assistance of parents. It may be difficult asking your wife's parents for favours, as you are not too intimate, but with the support and prodding coming from your wife, you take up the challenge. This brings to remembrance a close acquaintance whose wife had a background in Education Administration, Guidance and Counseling. Realizing that the wife had great potentials and having served the government for over fifteen years as a Teacher and Vice Principal, he suggested and agreed with the wife to set up a School. Immediately, the wife suggested that they seek the assistance of her mother to lease her block of six flats in the suburb of Lagos to them. The husband was reluctant to accede to this suggestion, saying he had funds to build a good structure, but it would take time! On analyzing the cost benefit, the husband eventually agreed. With this singular decision, the couple were able to secure their future. Now, they have three other nursery and primary schools around Lagos. As long as couples do not abuse opportunities and favours bequeathed on them by in-laws, such as soft loans, temporary use of properties and so on, the family will continue to be fortified exceedingly.

A marriage counsellor, Ololade Adesola, in a discussion had this to say. About in-laws, she says: *"In-laws need to give space and independence. Give advice but don't be offended if advice is not used. Give financial support only when asked, never offer. Do not take sides in quarrels. In fact, refuse to be involved except if it happens too often. Instead give advice about issues at a time when emotions have calmed. Pray, pray, pray without ceasing."*

About intimacy, she says: *"Intimacy is driven by mutual respect, a sense of security and safety. Physical gifts and romantic gestures do not have lasting effects."*

About where the husband can "miss it," she says: *"In Ephesians 5:22, we are told 'wives submit to your own husband'. Likewise, Ephesians 5:21 says: '...submitting to one another in the fear of God'. Therefore, mutual submission out of the fear of God is the basis of a wife's submission. A husband who doesn't practice mutual submission has missed it. The Bible in several places say honour your wife. This is the principle of sowing and reaping. To get honour, the husband must sow honour. If he doesn't honour his wife, the Bible says his prayer will not be answered."*

PRUDENCE KNOCKING AT THE HOMEFRONT

"Men are divided between those who are as thrifty as if they would live forever, and those who are extravagant as if they were going to die the next day."

Aristotle

One of the great concepts that will ensure a successful marriage is prudence on the part of both husband and wife. The two should see the relationship, not as a commercial relationship, whereby the wife mismanages funds being released by the husband, because she believes the husband is the bread winner, and he should always make funds available when needed, not minding the economic situation at hand. On the husband's part, taking advantage of the wife's corporate job to obtain loans to prosecute contracts that are not viable or profitable without any plan to refund, creates unnecessary tension in the relationship, as other family needs will suffer, such as children's upkeep, school fees, house maintenance and maybe vehicle maintenance. If you maintain a joint account, both couple must abide with the terms guiding the account. I experienced a situation whereby the mandate given to a corporate account of a couple was "any one can sign". The husband emptied the account within a month after a successful business year and relocated abroad, leaving the wife and two children behind! This is where trust comes in; husband and wife should be open when it comes to money issues and communicate appropriately so they both understand where the shoe pinches.

Someone was asking sometime ago if wives need to return the change outstanding on completion of purchases from house keeping allowances to their husbands. In as much as I feel this will not be necessary as the husband had taken the supposed amount off his budget, it is however necessary that the wife utilizes this change on things mutually useful to the couple and eventually the family.

When do wives ask for money or make additional request for funds? This should be done any time. As long as this is done politely, there should not be any friction. The husband should also explain gently why the request could not be met at the particular time and when it will be convenient. A lady narrated her frustration the other day, claiming that whenever she requested for money from her husband at bedtime, the husband claims it is too late and that they should discuss the following day. When she brings up her request early in the morning, the husband says it is too early as he is preparing for work and he has so many things cluttering his mind, and they will discuss on his return. The rigmarole continues unending! What we advise is for the wife to study the husband's mood and identify the right time to chip in her request.

When the couple is on a project, for instance, a building project, both have to know where to cut the fat, as all other expenses, such as school fees, house rent, power and gas bills will still be on the table. They should set their priorities right; what needs to wait and what should be done at the moment should be adequately spelt out and understood. The sacrifice is for the couple now that they are one in love, not for the wife alone.

Every travel needs to be planned, either local or international. There is the tendency to overspend if a budget is not put to it. A number of impulse purchases abound when on a journey and you may return home being out of purse. However, if well-planned with a budget, you will return home psychologically settled.

Encouragement is the watchword if any of the spouses experience a job loss. The wife or the husband has to be sensitive about their choice of words, in order not to trigger anger. The family finances will dwindle, but it will be necessary for the atmosphere at home to be peaceful also. Couples in this type of situation are advised to take on the next available job they are interested in to fill the gap. Some may have to reskill in order to take up new roles. For example, I remember in the course of my career, a Human Resources Manager that undertook safety courses in order to take a role as Safety Coordinator in an Oil Servicing Company, after losing his job as a result of downsizing in a manufacturing company. With this move, the family finances will be buoyed and it will serve as an eye opener to friends, relatives and other dependants that marriage is about being focused, setting priorities and overcoming challenges and not holding on in despair. We have had instances of wives putting pressure on their husbands to go back into paid employment because of initial challenges in their new business outfits. The advise is that having worked for a big company for several years, helping them go through thick and thin of their business, you should take the utmost strength to grow your own business to maturity. All businesses face challenges. If the need arises, approach banks, finance houses, wealthy friends and committed relatives, or tested business owners in your field of business. You will surely come out of "the dip". It is recommended that you order and read "The Dip" written by Seth Godin, a little book that teaches you when to quit and when to stick. Another area of prudence in marriage is in managing the fleet of cars you have acquired. You have to plan the use of the vehicles for every occasion, whether for school runs, business or domestic, as the case maybe. It is even advisable to hire a cab, or go on "Bolt" or "Taxify" once in a while, ensuring you also avoid "the surge" periods which can be very expensive. If you do not require a Driver for more than three months, hire one and dispose of him accordingly and carry on with your wife taking on the necessary driving. If you can afford the cost of school buses, register; if otherwise, align your movement with that of your children to enable them get to school on time and you to work appropriately.

When the children are in the kindergarten and primary schools, you will need a permanent house help, but as they get into the secondary school and higher institutions, you may only need a part-time helper, while the grown up children will fill the gap of the outstanding chores. This arrangement saves cost and you are able to divert resources to more rewarding aspects of family life.

Cutting your coat "according to your cloth," not "according to your size," applies when renting an apartment. If your company pays you ₦1 million per annum for accommodation, that does not mean you should hire an apartment of ₦1 million per annum. Couples should have in mind that rent will not be static, so they should be forward looking and see to what is manageable for the family in terms of accommodation and their purse now and in the nearest future. We have had cases of couples renting large apartments so as to impress their relatives and friends, but it turned out that they were unable to afford the rents in later years, thus moving to smaller and affordable apartments thereafter. Why not start small and finish big?

In a pre-retirement session I facilitated for a manufacturing company, some of the male participants were really agitated about how they can settle their wives on retirement. Our response was that men going on retirement should not see their wives as a problem. We are in a dynamic world and things change so rapidly. You can not give a lump sum to your wife to start a business and you feel you have "settled" her for life. So you do not expect her to ask you for any financial support again. When you take this route, you tend to brood conflict. What if you set up the business and it fails? You must be ready to support her in future endeavours. What we are saying in essence is that you do not have the premonition that you are settling your wife "for life"! You need to guide her in the business and give necessary advice and financial assistance continuously. If the business succeeds, all well and good, but if otherwise, you do not shift blame or search for who caused the problem, but pick your strategy and think of what next to go into. In my own experience, having had the knowledge of multiple streams of income over the years, I encouraged my wife to be involved in a number of small-scale businesses, ranging from sales of clothings, shoes and bags, to multilevel marketing – drugs, make-up, kitchen wares to wholesale of vegetable oil. At every point of review that we find one of the aspects not yielding results and unprofitable, we discuss and drop it. We had cases of customers purchasing on credit and not willing to pay and some did not pay in certain instances. The saving grace for my wife's profitability was the fact that she operated from home, rather than renting a shop or warehouse for her various goods.

From the foregoing, resources flowing from the husband ("Head of House") need to be managed and monitored continuously. You just have to prioritize to identify what works for you as a family. What works for other families may definitely not work for you, so you need to be at alert always.

Another major area where prudence knocks at the home front is in the area of the type of car to ride. Many couples at the early stage will like to purchase a vehicle that befits their status. Some believe that as long as they are able to access soft loans or long-term loans at their place of work, they should go for it! This is very good, but it needs to be thought through, as you need to consider the maintenance cost of the vehicle, including the availability of its spare parts. Also, as the family grows, you may require three cars at a go, may be one for business purposes, the other for school runs and another for the master's official use. This scenario has to be reviewed constantly, in the sense that you may have to collapse the car for school runs to also do the business trips. I had a friend in Lagos, Nigeria, who had a bus for school runs and also utilized it for his wholesale business for noodles and beer. He ensured that he aligned himself with his wife and bus driver so that the timing for the school runs or activities are kept. In other instances, some couples reduce their cars from two to just one by dropping the children in school early in the morning, go to work and register the children for after school lessons, so they can stay late in school till the parent's closing hours, when they are picked up. The case is easy for non-working mothers, as in my own case, having had the luxury of an official car as a Sales Manager, my wife was very comfortable using our car to do the school runs and do her small-scale business. However, as soon as my role changed and I had to drop the sales vehicle, I joined in the school trail, dropping the children off in school, going to work and releasing the vehicle to my wife for plans for the evening trip. This saved us a great deal of cost, instead of having a separate vehicle for my official use and another for school runs.

The staff bus opportunities in some companies assisted a great deal in saving cost for vehicle maintenance. Couples that find themselves in this situation have to be disciplined, in terms of keeping to schedules or the route plan of the buses. Or else they lose the essence of joining the staff bus, which is to enable you to get to work on time, as you have to leave home earlier than others. A great deal of work would have been achieved before other employees troop in for the day's job, just about the nick of resumption time.

Some other ways of "cutting the fat" in a marriage is for couples to discuss appropriately and decide on the type of house they want to build or buy. Depending on the sources of income, some may go for a mortgage, while some go for outright construction. In the days of yore, it was easy for couples to work in the city, rent a modest place but construct a retirement home in their home towns, which they move into at retirement from work in the city. However, things have changed considerably. With the rate at which rents are escalating in the cities, couples are now building in the suburbs of these cities! Though transportation could be a challenge, they believe cost of rent is manageably reduced. For example, in Lagos, Nigeria, people work in the city centres such as Ikeja, Marina, Lekki, but have houses in the suburbs such as Ibafo, Ikorodu, Epe, Ajah and Sangotedo. They take advantage of the Bus Rapid Transport (BRT) means of transportation, so as to get to work on time. Sometime ago, a friend who works as a driver in a private firm narrated how he had to live his home by 4:30am daily to catch the BRT in Ikorodu so as to get to Ikeja on Lagos Mainland by 7:00am. Likewise, those working on Lagos Island, Marina, Lekki, Ikoyi, Victoria Island, but living at Ajah, Sangotedo suburbs also have to leave home by 4:00am so as to get to work by resumption time, and avoid the traffic snarl. There was a video clip making the rounds on Whatsapp some months ago showing a dreadful hold up by 4:00 am in a Lagos suburb area. The voice over in the video screamed "Lagos no be your mate," indicating that you need to "respect" Lagos for its peculiar standards of living.

My usual advice to couples is that they should rent the houses they can afford and the moment they feel it is no longer affordable , they can move to an affordable one. It tells on your purse and your finances, not on what people will say or how people will perceive you. As regard the right place to live, you may want to save cost by living in the suburb, but when security is a challenge or vehicle maintenance continues to gulp a great deal of your finances, you will want to consider opportunities that abound in getting a modest accommodation in the city. This may be mortgage or long-term loans through finance houses or through cooperative societies.

COMMUNICATING RIGHTLY

"We are more interested in making others believe we are happy than in trying to be happy ourselves."

Francois Duc de la

Most couples communicate adequately during courtship; I dare say as pen pals, with all the jokes and laughter. However, this bond of relationship relaxes when couples get married and allow the vicissitudes of life to get the better of them. This happens because you get to know yourselves better now that you are living together. Some things you said during courtship and you laughed over may now get on the nerves of either of the spouses. Couples are to wake up early in the morning and have a word of prayer before going about their normal daily activities. Prayer is the key for a successful and lasting marriage, so it should be given great priority in family life.

In some traditions in Africa, the wife is expected to go to the husband's side and kneel down, then greet and hail him with his praise name. Thereafter, the husband heralds the entire family for prayers. As modernity has set in now, it is advisable that couples greet in their room and pray together immediately and thereafter invite other family members, children and relatives for prayers. There is the tendency for one of the couple to raise an eyebrow saying: "but we have just prayed" or "how many times are we going to pray?" The onus is on the husband to explain that the couple's prayer is different from the general prayer. Likewise, the couple's prayer should also take place at bedtime. This will lay a good foundation for a lasting marriage.

In some other instances, couples pick quarrels from the prayer aspect, one of the couple believing the other is not spiritual and saying his or her prayer separately or after the couple's prayer, going on to start another set of prayers. At this point, both couple have to understand what the issue really is. Nowadays, most churches and Evangelists send their Daily

Devotionals online, so a number of couples cash in on this to add to their prayers. So it is understandable when couples complete their joint prayer and thereafter go into their individual online Devotionals on their mobile apps. It is also advisable that a joint session is held at weekends when everyone is more relaxed and no one is rushing out to work.

Then the question goes: "Who is to phone check?" That is, who is to call while away from home, either at work or on a journey or a brief outing? Most couples disagree over this. Some wives believe the husband left them at home, so he should call to check how they are faring. On the other hand, the husband believes he is always too busy at work, so his wife should call to check on him. I dare say, this is just laxity, because before the advent of mobile phones, couples never had these arguments and they lived peaceably! What I encourage is that whoever is free to call should endeavour to carry out this task. In some organizations, you are only allowed to make or receive calls during lunch time. So, it may not be convenient to call at just anytime. Couples will just have to adjust their schedules accordingly.

Some wives form the habit of calling their husbands about closing time to ask for what he would like for dinner. Then a great deal of argument ensues, as regards what is available and otherwise. The best way to overcome this is to prepare an agreed timetable for food. Adequate notice will have to be duly communicated and agreed on any changes. This situation also dovetails into the housekeeping allowance at the wife's disposal. If a certain amount (x) has been on the table for some months, this may have to be reviewed upwards as a result of sprawling inflation and scarcity of some of the food items. The wife has to find a way to explain to the husband gently how expensive things are in the market. The moment couples understand market trends, they will manage their spending. A husband who is also asking for fresh fish, cow tail, snails and periwinkle garnished vegetable soup, will realize that he has to control his demands and watch his pockets, so as to be able to meet other family needs. With this, a new timetable will be drawn up.

Furthermore, communicating rightly entails some emotional intelligence, asking: "how will the other person feel with what I am about to say?" The moment you have the premonition that the other person will feel bad, will not take it lightly or will feel insulted, you have to desist from saying what you intend to say. Some troublesome wife or husband will want to spite the other person in the relationship, not minding the outcome. The scriptures encourage us to "follow peace with all men"(Hebrews 12:14). You must always create an atmosphere of peace around you and your spouse. You will be sending a good signal to your children about what an ideal environment should be in a marriage. This will help you from settling quarrels among your children and their spouses in old age. What we are saying in essence is that couples should not have the mindset of "paying back in his own coin", or having to respond to every comment made. There are a number of comments that you could easily overlook as soon as you know it is going to forment trouble or it portends unnecessary arguments.

There is the trend of ladies trying their best to accept all the insult from their husbands while raising children, only to commence trouble when the children are grown up and have left home. The wives call it "pay back time!" Believing that they could respond adequately to any negative comment raised by their husbands, this creates a tense atmosphere in their homes. This trend is avoidable, as long as issues are discussed and trashed out immediately they occur. There should not be any communication gap in marriage. Conscious effort must be made to ensure couples understand each other and avoid issues of conflict. So the couple does not miss the essence of living in their marriage, we refer them to what the Holy Scriptures tell us in Ephesians 5:21: "Submitting yourselves one to another in the fear of God." Thus, the husband honours the wife and vice versa. At the end, they both reap what they sow.

We have heard of cases of husbands welcoming their wives with uncouth words on returning from an outing, thus eliciting negative feedback from their wives. This leads to quarrelling and malice. With the traffic situation in our cities, where people spend hours on the road, missing appointments and unable to keep to plans, there is the tendency to arrive home late from work and from events. What we always advise is for couples to pray for their going out and coming in. Telecommunication network issues may not help matters, thus raising a great deal of anxiety. Colossians 4:6 (KJV) is instructive at this point, which says: "Let your speech be always with grace, seasoned with salt that ye may know how ye ought to answer every man." A Christian marriage should not be fraught with negative thoughts and comments. There should be mutual trust culminating in psychological safety in the marriage, fortifying a strong bond.

WE ARE WIRED DIFFERENTLY

"In spite of everything I still believe that people are really good at heart"
Anne Frank

"The nature of Men is always the same; it is their habits that separate them"

Confucius

Have you ever noticed that the way a first born behaves is quite different from that of a last born child in a family? This also has its various colourations when you consider the gender. A male child as a first born in a family tends to be highly resourceful, responsible for his younger ones, directing and guiding them so that they do not derail in life. He strives so much so that his siblings can match his achievements. Back in the days, in the traditional setting, as soon as the first born completes his university education and gets a good job, he immediately becomes responsible for the education of his other siblings. Some even move along with him to his new apartment and live there. From there, they also find their bearing in life. For the male coming as a last born, they tend to be lackadaisical, thinking things will just work out. So they need to be monitored continuously and checked so that they can be on the right track in life and on any assignment given. Socially, they tend to be friendly though rebellious. This in turn ensures respect for them as they shower him with love at all times, as all his senior ones see him as their pet, while he gets gifts of clothes, shoes, wristwatches and so on. With this background, a last born male child turns out to be a giver and friendly in marriage. As for a female child coming as a first child, you find a very responsible lady, serving as a coordinator of her younger ones, ensuring tasks are completed, a sole finisher, very neat and ultimately a lavish giver. She influences her siblings rather than coerce them, as you may find with the male child.

The female child as last born takes a cue from her elder sister, takes after her behaviour and tries to imbibe her idiosyncracies, in terms of dressing, fashion and gait. She is also a giver, having a lot flowing to her. She will have a great deal to flow to others within her environment and fold. In terms of domestics, the female last born may be rebellious, as she believes all chores are being passed on to her and she may be overwhelmed. Especially, if she has male siblings who will not pity her, as they see household chores as that of ladies!!

From the foregoing, therefore, we realize that coming into marriage, we are already wired differently, with varied background socially, spiritually and economically. This calls for mutual respect and understanding in the relationship. A friend who grew up under a strict father as a first born, with the background of keeping to time for every occasion, got married to a lady who was a last born and was used to being guided and instructed by her parents and siblings in most things. There was a lot of friction in the early days of their marriage, because the wife could hardly cope with the headmaster approach of her spouse. She complained of the husband being too formal, saying we should be out of this house in one hour, not minding all the household chores she has to go through, such as cleaning the house, taking care of their two children, bathing them and feeding them! The husband just had his bath, sits in the sitting room and screams at the wife about not wanting to go late for the event, whether church service or a social event. The wife scampers here and there, confused, complaining and uncoordinated. Eventually, they get out of the house late and ultimately arrive at the event far beyond the expected time. This unpalatable situation went on for years until the husband realized that he could help with taking care of the children, while the wife gets other things ready. Instead of shouting out orders, he will usher the children into the bathroom, get them to shower and dress them up. He then feeds them and they all await his wife to round-up things. With this they were able to overcome any anomalies about arriving at events on time. If you come from a very strict background, though it is good to pass this on to the next generation, it is necessary to study the situation at hand.

There was also a case of a couple who traveled to Europe and before returning to Nigeria, they decided to do some shopping. While the husband being a first born wrote the list of things to buy for his siblings, the wife only wrote the list of things to buy for her children and the house. The wife then queried the husband on the need to buy things for his siblings, as he could utilize the funds to buy more things for the children and household. More so, the supposed siblings have the privilege of traveling to Europe from time to time. The husband being very mature and because he understood his wife's background, had to explain that they were taught right from childhood to always look out for each other. With this explanation, the wife got to understand the husband better and never raised an eyebrow in future travels whenever the husband did extended family shopping.

Talking of the extended family too, some husbands come from large families, and have been exposed to the retinue of family members while growing up. It is advisable that the husband allows the wife, either during courtship or early in the marriage, to have a cordial relationship with some of these family members. This will further enhance intimacy in the relationship. There was the scenario of a newly-married couple who attended a family event and the wife realized that the husband had to get up on the arrival of every aunty or uncle to the event, to greet and introduce his new wife. After a while, the wife got nervous and exploded, saying: "Do we have to greet everyone? I am tired of getting up every now and then!" It took the calmness of the husband to manage the situation. In some other clime, the wife could walk out and go and sit down in the car till the end of the event, which could be detrimental to the relationship and the extended family. In my own instance, I had intimated my spouse with my hood of siblings during courtship, making her psychologically stable. Likewise, before marriage, with the insistence of my dad, after all was set, I had to drive down to Ado-Ekiti with my spouse, to introduce her to my aged grandmother, uncles and aunties. And on the way back, we stopped at Ibadan to see another aunty. With this development, till date, my wife is able to flow into any family event or associate with any family member from my end. This also gave me the impetus to delve freely with my spouse's family as there was nothing to hide, but a lot to learn from both families in terms of tradition and good quality family life.

In a relationship, some are wired to keep a retinue of friends from courtship days, deep into the marriage and old age, while some will want to cut off or avoid some of their friends as soon as they get married. As long as there is no bad influence, friendship should continue for a lifetime. You never know when you will need each other! I can attest to my wife's childhood friend being instrumental to the employment of two of our children. Another was available as a "live in" attendant while my wife had to undergo a surgery, as I was only able to visit the hospital just a few hours per day during her three-week sojourn there. As for my own friends, they have always been at my beck and call in good and bad times. I remember one time I needed an SUV to serve as my children's school bus and I spoke to one of my friends, Ikenna, who had one that he used sparingly. He released the van to me within a week, with both of us agreeing to payment terms. This vehicle served as a great relief to myself and my wife. With this, my wife cherished the essence of keeping good and reliable friends from early to deep married life. In terms of our affecting other people's lives too, I remember a friend who was going abroad for further studies and was having challenges completing his ticket fare and he wanted to dispose of his heavy duty generator. Meanwhile, we had a friend who had just moved to his new house in a highbrow area of Lagos. I contacted him and got him and the earlier mentioned friend to negotiate. It was a good buy for the former. With this, my friend was able to get his ticket on time. We are still the best of friends – friendship of about 30 years!

I remember my wife impacting a family friend's life by making her mini car available for him to perfect his driving. With this, he was able to take up an Executive Sales Manager's job in a pharmaceutical company in Lagos. How are couples wired when it comes to trust? While some husbands take things for granted, the wives will not leave anything to chance based on their experience and exposure while growing up. A case in point was a lady who at the age of twelve was informed by her father to prepare the guest room in their house, as they will be receiving a visitor the following day. Unknown to her, the father was bringing in a second wife alongside a new addition (baby) to the family! With this in mind, as a wife, this lady was suspicious of her husband's official relationships. The husband, who is very jovial and takes things for granted, was a Sales Manager with one of the manufacturing companies in Lagos. On one occasion, he met this old classmate, a lady who had a pharmacy store and sold some of the products of the manufacturing company in her store. They renewed their friendship and the Sales Manager arranged for the children of both families to meet just to have some fun. He explained this to his wife at home, thinking that his wife will understand easily, but the wife reluctantly released her two children, ages seven and nine. On another occasion, the lady pharmacist called to inform the Sales Manager friend that her daughter had been yearning to see her friends again and will like to come over to spend a weekend with them. The Sales Manager agreed to this and told his wife about the development, but the wife received the news with so much coldness as opposed to the excitement of the husband and the children! This not withstanding, the Sales Manager husband brought the girl for the weekend. The children had fun and enjoyed themselves, but the Sales Manager's wife, based on her childhood experience was of the premonition that her husband was bringing in a child he had out of wedlock home with style! With this cold war during the weekend, this jovial husband learnt how to draw the line in renewing old friendship! He continued with the official relationships, but never at the family level.

HUMBLE BEGINNINGS

"There will be no greater ones if there were no little ones"

George Herbert

"I awoke one morning and found myself famous"

George Gordon

That Chairman of a multinational company that you view with so much awe, had humble beginnings. Likewise, that Bishop, Director in a government establishment, as well as that State Governor! Therefore, in selecting a spouse you do not overlook potentials, which is the key to success and what drives people into future opportunities. You hear our youthful ladies saying: "I cannot marry 'a starter' who is just beginning life!" The questions to ask are: "Does he have a job? Is he focused? Does he have a plan for both of you? Is he ready to propose to you or he is scared or jittery when you talk of marriage?" Someone I know began his career as a junior Accountant in a finance house and his fiancé was always nagging, because salaries were meagre and irregular. She just took the relationship as a stroll in the park! While the man was focused, studying hard and obtaining professional certifications, that stood him in great stead for better jobs, the lady who was a classroom Teacher kept on looking down on his fiancé. Unfortunately, she got pregnant and while both extended families met to sort out issues of marriage, the lady was adamant, saying she could not marry the man. She had it behind her mind that the partner could not sustain her in marriage with his kind of job. Eventually, it was resolved that the lady would keep the child and the man endeavoured to be responsible for the child. Some ten years down the line, having been communicating only via phone and the child kept away from the father, the couple met at a business event and the lady was surprised to see the man as the keynote speaker, with aides accompanying him as well as a police escort. The man had set up his own business management firm, with a retinue of employees, consulting for private and public sector organizations. The couple could only exchange pleasantries and go their different ways, but the fact still remains that the lady would have learnt a bitter lesson and will not advise any other lady to go the route she went as she remained a single mother, but the man was happily married.

This situation keeps occurring in relationships; as the men are ready to grow the ladies, see them through higher institutions, build businesses for them, so that they can be psychologically and financially stable in marriage. On the other hand, the ladies find it difficult to see the bigger picture or see the potential in the man, by supporting his humble endeavours, so it thrives gradually to greater accomplishments!

We although have some scenarios of ladies who stood by their husbands to build a virile family. The following story lends credence to this. It is the story of a man working with his Higher National Diploma in one of the government departments and dating a lady working as an officer in one of the commercial banks. The lady saw great potentials in the man and encouraged him to take professional examinations in banking. The man took this advice, studied hard and passed the necessary papers to qualify him for an officer role in another bank. The couple got married and thrived exceedingly in their careers. The husband resigned after some years to set up a supermarket and bakery business, while the wife joined later after three years to add a quick service restaurant to the business. With all the support for each other in the early days before marriage, couples should be able to respect themselves more when they remember their humble beginnings.

MANAGING YOUR SUCCESS

"The doorstep to the temple of our wisdom is a knowledge of our own ignorance."

Charles Spurgeon

"Knowledge comes, but wisdom lingers."

Alfred Lord Tennyson

You have been given a political appointment. You are no longer accessible to your family members, to your friends and former colleagues! You have moved your residence from a suburb to a highbrow area of the city; you no longer want your friends to know your itinerary. You bought a new car, making a second one for the family; you feel your siblings should not know! You won a target set at work and the reward was a trip to Dubai for a fortnight and you chose to hide it from your other friends and siblings. You were promoted from middle level manager to senior level manager or Director in your organization; you do not want to share this joy with your siblings or former classmates. Your daughter or son is getting married, then you select few friends and family members to inform. You make statements such as: "I cannot invite everybody in the family!" The passing out of your son from the military school was announced on the national news and you still feel your relatives should be kept in the dark!

All these just show what premium you lay on people — those who have made a difference in your life. That is why this book really deals with scenarios in an African setting. In as much as some of us believe that we do not care what people say, we need to remember that at every stage in life, you will need people, either family members, friends, old classmates, former colleagues and other people that come your way in life. Those siblings you are avoiding maybe highly networked and you will be worried that everywhere you turn, you come across their acquaintances. With the strong aid of telecommunication, we have the Closed Universal Group (CUG) system set up for large organizations and families by Telcos, the Whatsapp Groups, the Zoom Calls, Microsoft teams, Google meet and Telegram, all in a bid to keep people together and build strong bonds. Unfortunately, some family members hide under the guise of being busy and avoid or cherry pick these groups or set ups, forgetting that they will leave those jobs one day and they will come back to the family they have avoided for camaraderie for their future days of celebration, maybe children's wedding, birthday celebrations, funeral ceremonies of elderly ones in the family and so on. These persons will become elders in the extended families, but will not be regarded as elders in the real sense of the word in the African setting, as their behaviour has not portrayed this noble nomenclature.

Some of these nonchallant behaviours split and destroy families that had earlier been the cynosure of all eyes and envy of society. When the so-called new found friends and acquaintances come along with authentic information of your family members that you are not aware of, you need to take this with regal silence and equanimity so as not to portray your siblings as ignorant.

A great deal lies with the menfolk when they get married to still maintain their closeness to their siblings, as their wives will be held responsible for any haughtiness on their part. Likewise, the wives have to ensure that the unity and camaraderie they met in the family is sustained; no matter what heights they reach in their careers or level they get to in the society. This act of humility will surely breed much respect for the wives. The additional reward is peace of mind and they will have nothing to hide or be scared of. My mum used to warn me to desist from telling lies, because if you tell a lie, you will need to look for ten additional lies to cover the first lie!

Even the Europeans we tend to copy cherish their family life and regard their close relatives! I remember a trip to Sofia, Bulgaria, for a programme and one of the ladies serving as our host was celebrating her 40th birthday. She had a lavish party and invited some of us from Nigeria. During the course of the party, she introduced us to some of her friends and relatives saying she had to give them a month's notice because she cherished them a great deal as they grew up on the mountains together. All of them were scattered in the cities of Bulgaria, such as Verna, Sofia, Tarnovo and Plovdiv, in high positions in multinational organizations! They still took time out to share the moment of joy with their childhood friends.

OUTSTATION MANOUVRES

"Travel, in the younger sort, is a part of education, in the elder, a part of experience."

Francis Bacon

"There is no pleasure in travelling, and I look upon it more as an occasion for spiritual testing."

Albert Camus

You want the money, so you should be able to sacrifice! When couples find themselves in situation whereby one member has to be away from home for a long time in order to fend for the family, either by way of short or long time assignments or even permanent postings, a discussion has to be held and firm decisions taken.

During the course of a couple's career, the husband may be posted out of base, such as from Lagos to Enugu for weeks. The man on his own part will have to make arrangement for finances at home to be unbridled, likewise communication. However, what we find in some cases is that some men get carried away with the comfort of the hotel accommodation and the allowances, and go on a spending spree and forget their families. When their wives call for financial support, they tend to be aggressive and end up sending pittance back home. This is where communication breaks down and love grows cold between couples. On the other hand, we have men who will take advantage of being away from home to be more spiritual during the lonely periods in the hotel rooms. Such men will also endeavour to call their family members regularly and save part of their allowances to buy goodies for the children on the way back home. I remember in our days, we ensured we paid visits to Ariaria market in Aba to buy clothing materials for the family, and whenever we traveled to the North ,it was certain we would return with packs of "Kilishi", "Danmbu Nanma" and "Suya", which were varieties of meat delicacies. Some wives even go to the extent to ask: "when are you traveling again?"

However, some couples in their early married life do not enjoy these movements. A wife kept on complaining that her husband was kept away for too long; even though she had more funds to spend , she believed the availability of her husband mattered. She complained that she could not enjoy the companion of her husband while on outings as other friends do! The husband had a running battle convincing her that it was the sacrifice they had to pay, for him to have a successful career.

From time to time, there were cases where husbands were transferred permanently to new locations. The man in such situation will have to decide what is convenient for the family. He needs to consider how easy it will be for the children's schooling if the whole family is moved to a new location, and if the new environment is more conducive than the current town or city in terms of security. For example, in our days, if you were posted out of Lagos to anywhere in Nigeria, in most cases, you had to leave the family behind or as work permitted. The wives had to manage this situation with constant communication and determination to keep the home front comfortable and peaceful. At that moment the wife plays the role of husband and wife! She takes the children to school, clinic, to visit grandparents, takes the car to technicians, and ensures all utilities at home are working top notch!

While Lagosians leave their family on ground, what we had in our days with a few exception is for men posted permanently to Lagos to move their families down and make it a base or launching pad for any other posting. The wives have to support their husbands as this assists his psychological safety. If the home front is comfortable, then he will be able to put in his best at work, culminating in greater achievements and promotions in his chosen career.

There was a complaint from a lady who visited me at home as we lived in the same estate, saying her husband stays too late at work, leaves home very early, even at weekends and was always at work! I had to counsel her that her husband was in his early to mid-career, whereby he had to throw himself into the career, and fight for his shirt as a team player, during this make or break period! She sobbed, saying it might take a long time, but I assured her that she should sacrifice by taking charge of the home front and she would reap the reward. Within a spate of two years, this same husband got a promotion at work and got a cross posting to South Africa (Durban)! The lady was highly elated to give me this news when it happened. That is the blessing you get when you support your husband. The family has since moved ahead to Australia, then to Indonesia, then to Malaysia and to Singapore, where they reside currently. I could have visited the family in my short stay in Johannesburg in October 2016, if not for incongruent work schedules. "It is a small world," as the saying goes!

SEPARATIONS AND ITS EFFECTS

"I am the master of my fate, I am the Captain of my soul."

William Ernest Henley

"A day, an hour of virtuous liberty, Is worth a whole eternity in bondage."

Joseph Addison

Apart from the harrowing effect on the female partner, the children suffer tremendously when couples decide to separate as a result of irreconcilable differences. Couples must try their utmost best to ensure they do not fall into this devilish trap, which occurs because of interference from friends, associates, relatives and vicissitudes of life. As the scripture says: "With God nothing shall be impossible!" All issues emanating from a marriage relationship must be laid at God's table, with fervent prayers, to avoid each one going their separate ways. Some couples will brag, saying: "leave us alone for now, we are just separated not divorced." They forget to realize the legal and scriptural implication, talk less of the adverse effect on their innocent children.

Apart from the love gone cold between the couple, the children tend to have soft spot for whoever they are staying with. If the mother is in custody of the children, they will love her exceedingly, as they see her as the all in all, even though the father sends money for tuition, clothing and feeding to the mother regularly. A more unfortunate situation can occur when the mother feeds them with negative stories about their father and his relatives. However, if the husband has custody of the children, he may not enjoy so much love from the children, as they keep on asking for their mother, or the time they will be able to visit and spend time with her. This has a psychological setback for the man, as he sees himself shuttling two homes and spending indiscriminately at times!

We witness a great deal of irrational behaviour emanating from the separated couple as well as the children. On the father's part, he becomes jittery whenever the children mention their mother and tends to vent his anger on them at any time. This makes the children timid and unable to say what is on their mind, thus affecting their social and academic life. As for the mother, she will continuously be on edge, seeing every lady as a competitor trying to take her place, so she responds harshly in her communication. While others find it difficult to interact as they see themselves as single mothers, some complain of not having enough funds to take care of the children, blaming the separated husband for his irresponsible behaviour. The children witness this and take sides with their mother, not knowing the deep facts of the matter.

There was a case of a separated couple where the husband from time to time will arrange for the estranged wife to come along with the children to an eatery; he takes them out and returns them at an agreed time. This situation occurred severally and the husband's relatives showered encomiums on the wife for taking care of the children and always dressing them up with good and fashionable clothes. However, on this fateful day, on another planned outing, the woman decided to surprise the husband, for he had not given her funds to buy clothes for the children for some time and as a result of obvious ego, she refused to ask. So she dressed the children, boys of ages 5 and 6, up in singlets and boxers and drove straight to the expected meeting point. While they were on the way, the children kept asking for their dresses. She responded that their father was "bringing them new clothes," ,so there was no need to wear any dress till they saw their father. On arrival at the eatery, the father approached the wife's car to pick the children up, but was surprised that they were meagerly dressed. Not wanting to make a fuss, he got the message and drove the children to a nearby shop to buy new clothes for them! With this scenario, the enstrangement deepens and of course, the reconciliation becomes more difficult. The children feeling the brunt of this ugly situation, eventually grow up to be divided in their thoughts.

In the case where the man goes on to remarry, the situation becomes more difficult for the children. They find it uneasy to warm themselves to the heart of the new wife, who may see the elderly children as unsupportive, depending on where they reside. When the children get married, they have to convince their spouses to adapt to the idiosyncracies of shuttling and managing both ends. Mainly, the onus lies on the husband in the new marriage to make sure that things work and do not go the way of his parents!

RAISING GODLY CHILDREN

"Parents with insights usually raise kids that are secure, fulfilled, relaxed, free to forge out ideas and to think."

Chuck Swindoll

We do not want to clone our children, but having seen and experienced life, we ought to guide them in the path of truth to succeed in life. 3 John 4 says: "I have no greater joy than to hear that my children walk in truth." What we sow, we will surely reap! We should imbibe in our children the fear of God, by engaging them in prayers and family Bible study sessions; ensuring they keep to attendance of church services and programmes. It is not enough to attend church services, our children must be involved in church activities, such as youth programmes, the brigade, choir, the band or choral groups. With this, they are forever present in God's vineyard, having good intentions and interacting with age mates in a spirit-filled manner.

At the home front, parents should endeavour not to pitch their children against themselves or play favourites. The moment this evil is allowed to trend it may continue throughout the lifetime of the siblings, thus breeding bad blood as the family expands. We as parents should not feed our children with stories that do not unite the family, should not create perceived enemies for them, or tell them to avoid certain relatives you had misunderstanding with while growing up. Let them lead their lives and form their opinions of people accordingly. That is the essence of the quality education you spent so much money upon. By the time your children graduate and start behaving like pagans, then the whole purpose of their education is defeated. Our children should be raised to honour their father and mother as the Holy Bible teaches; this does not mean biological parents only. We need to inculcate in them the respect of elders of any tribe, creed and religion. With this, they will be able to wade through life's maze easily, and they will be acknowledged as children of God. A case in point while growing up was a day I visited one of my brothers who got newly-married and was living in the heart of Lagos, in one of the flats in a building of four flats. On arriving at the building, I met one of my old classmates and on learning that his co-tenant was my brother, he was full of praises for him, showering him with encomiums and affirming that my brother has maintained the family's Christian tenets which he displayed by respecting all other elderly tenants in the building, attending to their needs when required and supporting the estate and community responsibly.

My visit portrays the continuous support required by parents and relatives alike to couples after marriage. We should still visit to check on the type of life they live. Though it may not be as frequent as we may want to, but we should create time for "flying visits". When passing through their area, we can stop over to say hello. We are Africans and we do not have to announce our visits every time. With the advent of the mobile phone, we can make calls to check how they are faring, even when they get too busy to call. We should not take offense; we should call. This positive behaviour will be passed on to the next generation, which makes communication seamless within the larger family. I can recall one of my sisters telling our mother that: "My Brother calls me, even if I do not call him, he does not believe in exchange of calls!" Of course, that should be the spirit.

Godly children do not have a glossary of "tit-for-tat"; pay him back in his own coin, or "law of karma", which is definitely unchristian. Of course, they will go through tests, get bruised, but build character. They should be guided by what Solomon tells us in Proverbs 4:23: "Guard your hearts with all diligence, for out of it flows the issues of life." Also, they should have behind their minds the words of Jim Elliot: "wherever you are be all there. Live to the hilt every situation you believe to be the will of God." With these our children will live a purpose-driven life and they will be able to attest to the fact that the life they live leads them towards a satisfying and meaningful future, while communicating a standard of moral purity. Thereby building a strong faith to wade through challenges of life and stand in the raging storms.

Our children should be raised to imbibe the tenets of delayed gratification. Though we are in the days of faster internet and artificial intelligence, they should be advised to exercise patience in whatever endeavours they find themselves.

Selflessness will be a great virtue to instill in Godly children. They should not expect payment for every service. For instance, an engineer in a manufacturing company can organize Mathematics or Physics lessons for students studying for O'Level in an estate on Saturdays free of charge.

Children should be raised to assist whoever, whenever, especially when those blue chip positions come, not only when in government. Surely, they are going to be exposed to great requests from siblings, friends, relatives and neighbours, as well as non-relatives (strangers).They need to be good Samaritans wherever they can, and preachers of the scriptures in character and deed as commanded by Jesus and recorded by Matthew in chapter 28:18-20. Couples should ensure their adolescent children register in and complete the discipleship programmes available in their churches. This will enable them to yearn to be more like Jesus Christ rather than just saying: "I want to make heaven." When you become more like Christ, heaven will come as a consequence.

In the disciple classes, participants are taught to develop Christ-like character and qualities, such as humility and being correctable, as well as the ability to pray rightly.

As a participant in the discipleship class of my parish church, St. Jude's Anglican Church, Omole, Lagos, which runs a robust programme, I was able to take away the acronym for praying, which has guided my prayer life, in relation to the inference of the Bible that we should not pray amiss. The acronym learnt was A.C.T.S., which stands for "Adoration", "Confession", "Thanksgiving", "Supplication". With this in mind, for anyone leading a prayer session or having a quiet time, you will be focused and direct in your prayers.

SECRET STORIES OF OLD

"To you it has been given to know the secrets and mysteries of the kingdom of Heaven, but to them it has not been given."

Matt. 13: 1

"The proper study of mankind is man."

Alexander Pope

Surely, there must be an intimate bond between couples and their acquaintances. This intimacy will be oiled by sharing information, secrets and old stories that have an impact on their relationships. With this, trust is enhanced as the wife will be surprised that so much is being confided in her and this also applies to the husband. The sacrifice and love revealed in these secrets and old stories portend a long-lasting relationship for the couple as neither will want to put a clog in the wheel of progress of the vibrant relationship.

The saying goes that: "If you want to gossip your boss, tell your wife." That is the extent of trust a man should have in his wife, as his wife will always keep the bond sacrosanct. Others will inform their own trusted friends, thus leading to change in perception, even if they do not go on to reveal the secret. A number of secrets and old stories that have shaped relationships over the years will be shared so as to encourage current and future marriage relationships.

After over twenty years of marriage, I told my wife that I have been able to manage her appropriately from the outset of our relationship because of what my father-in-law told me about her. My father-in–law had told me that my wife had proved to be very intelligent from her youth and I should, as a much mature and elderly person be able to manage her precociousness rather than take offence! This revelation prodded a great surprise from my wife and she was so awed, saying: "My Dad told you that? No wonder you do not get annoyed easily nor keep malice with me. You are a darling!"

Thank God that the intimacy is getting stronger by the day, even in our twenty-eighth year!

The 1980 Ogunpa flood in Ibadan, southwest Nigeria, nearly took the life of my wife, her twin brother and her mum, while returning from school. The mum's car got stuck in the extension of the flood in a high plain; thank God for two hefty men who braved the odds to carry them through the floods to safety. Hundreds of people died in this flood and I still continue to appreciate God for saving my wife's life, her mum, brother and my cherished mother-in-law. This story narrated by my wife after ten years of marriage, makes me love her the more, as I would not imagine what my life could have been with another woman!

Revealing your dexterity or hidden skills enhances intimacy in marriage. I remember purchasing a talking drum sometime, bringing it home and hanging it in our sitting room. My wife just saw it as a piece of decoration, not until the day I brought it down and played it to the amazement of my wife and children. I had to tell them that I learnt the skill through my class teacher, Elder Festus Onigbinde, in primary school, Staff School, University of Ife. Festus Onigbinde was multi-talented. He taught us how to play the talking drum, participated in the marching band at morning assemblies, taught us baseball and football. As we all know, he was the Technical Manager of the Nigerian National Football team, the Green Eagles, for some years.

A friend narrated to his wife after fifteen years how he shuttled Aba for months before his wedding to buy clothing materials at Ariaria market, sewed nice shirts and brought them back to Lagos through night bus at weekends. The wife exclaimed: "You did all that to make us comfortable?" This made the wife respect the husband more, and she was consistent in maintaining a strong bond in the now twenty years relationship.

Another friend of mine informed me how he boosted the intimate relationship with his wife, when he revealed to her after twelve years in marriage, the way he stopped over in the hospital every morning for one month, in order to supervise the cleaning of his mother-in-law who had a terminal ailment. This was two years into the marriage; his wife was heavily pregnant so she could not be so much involved in the hospital visits and he had instructed the hospital staff not to tell his wife about his movements. The wife jumped up and screamed:" You did all that for mama? God will continue to surprise you exceedingly!" The marriage has since grown stronger and the wife has extended this same love to her mother-in-law.

Some wives also tend to wonder why their husbands are so close to some friends or relatives. This unfolds stories of old and in some instances, secrets that have been hidden over the years. I remember vividly my wife, surprisingly, asking why I am so close to one of my senior cousins, Brother Akinlabi Fayinminnu, who is now a Reverend gentleman with the Anglican Communion in the city of Ibadan, southwest Nigeria. I had to narrate the story of how my cousin walked me to school in my kindergarten days while I lived with my grandmother at Ado-Ekiti, bought snacks for me at lunch time and also walked me back home to my grandparents' house. Also, this strong relationship continued when I got to secondary school, Christ's School, Ado-Ekiti. We were in the same House (Mason) and he was two years ahead of me. Brother Akinlabi ensured I was serious with my studies and encouraged me as necessary. Fortunately, on my moving to Ibadan in 2017, we have been in the same Diocese and have been worshiping together in the same Bodija Archdeaconry. So it was so easy for me to invite him to officiate at my wife's 50th birthday in 2018. He also officiated at my daughter's wedding at All Soul's Church, Bodija, in 2021. With all these, my wife has discovered that the intimate relationship with my cousin has to be respected.

A friend narrated the old story of how he bought his first television set, a black and white box type in the late 1980s with the help of a senior friend to his wife, after fifteen years in marriage. The wife was always asking why he was so close to Bayo. The husband narrated how he was working in a lonely Agricultural Institute in Ilesa, southwest Nigeria, with vast farmlands, classrooms, staff quarters and animal husbandry areas. At close of work everyday, they returned to the Staff Quarters, alongside his friend Bayo, had dinner, discussed and narrated stories, and thereafter went to bed. This routine continued for six months and the husband maintained that he felt "shut out" of the world on the farm site. He believed he needed to listen and update himself with the latest news in the country. So he narrated his need to his friend Bayo, saying he needed to buy a television set costing ₦60, but could only raise ₦10! Bayo decided to lend him the ₦60, payable in six instalments. By the next day, Bayo had released the funds and boom, the television set was installed in the husband's apartment. So he could watch the news, football matches and latest music ratings as at then. Since Bayo and this friend have moved on to different endeavours, they have always kept in touch and shared joyful moments as necessary. This has increased the love of my friend's wife for her husband and friend, cherishing their humble beginnings.

Another area of discourse in terms of secrets and stories of old in marriage is how couples or their parents were able to finance their education and see them through school. While some had a smooth sail, the story was not the same for others. For instance, in our days, in the higher institution, we had colleagues who had to go home few days in the month to help their parents in the family business, so as to gather enough funds to sponsor their studies. A friend, Gbemisola from Saki in southwest Nigeria, had to travel home monthly from University of Ife to monitor the logistics of his aunty and guardian's yam flour business. The aunty had a large yam flour business , with goods that had to be transported to Ibadan, Lagos and to the West Coast, as far as Ouagadougou (Wagga) in Burkina Faso. He was able to gain some funds from these assignments to pay his tuition and boarding fees throughout his four-year course at the university. As graduation present, the aunt bought Gbemisola a Volkswagen Beetle car! It was a rare and unique reward for a fresh graduate in our days. By the time my friend narrated this story to his wife years into their marriage, it was a moment to cherish and respect her husband and also love this aunty.

Another friend was about missing his final year exams in the university as a result of scarcity of funds to complete his project. The mother packed all her trinkets and asked my friend to take them to a particular goldsmith and dealer in Idumota, downtown Lagos Island. Within three days, the trinkets were sold and enough funds raised for my friend to complete his project and sustain himself till the end of the session. Great respect goes to this mother who sacrificed all her luxury for the sake of her son! Of course, my friend's wife continues to hold her mother-in-law in high esteem!

CHALLENGES ABOUND
"For better for worse, For richer for poorer, In sickness or in health"

I am very sure we are familiar with this quote, which has been the marriage vow for couples down the ages! A number of couples say this out of compulsion at the wedding solemnization, and do not act in real life the tenets of this vow in their marriages. Few years into the marriage, you hear of unending quarrels as a result of promiscuity, lack of perseverance and endurance during challenges and so many unpalatable cases that point to the fact that couples no longer respect their marriage vows. Couples that had hitherto been enjoying a peaceful marriage, suddenly turn out to live as strangers in the home just because of simple financial challenges or simple disagreement on issues. Whereas they should have had in mind the popular saying: "The roots grow deep when the winds are strong."

If each partner in the relationship is determined to make the marriage work, it will, not minding the challenges that arise. You pray through this problem and pray the challenges away. You have to look back to the days you had been overcoming other challenges together, without any interference.

There was a story of a family some few years ago where the husband lost his job in a door manufacturing company in Lagos, Nigeria. The man was instrumental to the success of the company as he presented great and unique designs of doors which yielded high turnover and profit to the company. Within three months, the effect of the loss of job took its toll on the family's finances. Meanwhile, the wife, a high school teacher, supported the partner for sometime but started complaining later that he was lazy, that he did not want to take up any other job and that he depended on her earnings. So she stopped preparing meals for the husband. On the other hand, what the partner was planning was to get sponsors, so that he could manufacture his own doors, through contract arrangement or production. The wife was not patient enough. There was communication breakdown and they lived as strangers and kept malice in the home. This affected the children and they sometimes asked their mother: "Mummy why are you always frowning at home?" She in turn will be aggressive and scold the children accordingly. Later the wife decided to go into event and party catering at weekends, to augment her salary. The husband offered to help in carrying out deliveries at events and also convey casual staff when required with his vehicle. Seeing that the husband has stretched forth an olive branch, the wife now was ready to listen to him, and they decided to have a heart-to-heart talk outside the house, at a fast food restaurant. The husband was able to lay his plans about securing a loan for designing and producing flush doors and selling to construction companies. Even though doors are part of the later fixtures in a building, he gets paid on time and had commenced the repayment of his loans. He mentioned that he was going to continue the payment of the school fees of the children. The wife was elated and they prayed together, hoping things will turn out for good. Three months down the line, the wife could experience that the husband was doing well as his business had picked up, with orders from various construction companies. However, the wife noticed that the husband was always putting on designer shirts and shoes with world class names such as "Texen", "Gucci", "Raphael", "Giorgio Buttini"and "Vera Cudio". She complained that it was expected that her husband should lie low by going for cheaper alternatives so as to save cost. The husband made her to understand that he had always maintained this standard and he would not want to cheapen himself. As long as he was able to meet his obligations, all will be well. On the long run, the couple was able to overcome their challenges, with better understanding of each other through communication and determination to make the relationship work.

Another area couples face challenges is when problem is seen, not as "our family problem", but as "your family problem". When issues come up in your in-law's family, you need to be involved and support them to the best of your abilities, as long as you are aware, or you are not informed of recent happenings or extent of the problem. I recall the case of a housemaid we got through a popular agent who ran an agency for securing and contracting househelps from Benin Republic to Lagos and its environs. Unknown to us, the lady had chronic hepatitis! This was however known to the agent! After staying with us for a few days, complaining of weakness at times, we taught it was the effect of the stress of traveling from Cotonou to Lagos. After a week, she felt better and we sent her to my mother-in-law at Ibadan. Within three weeks, it was reported that she was always reluctant to do any work in the house, as she did not want to overstretch herself. My mother-in-law complained of this anomaly, as she could not be paying for the services of a lazy house help! A few days later, Mama called to say the lady slumped and gave up the ghost and was lying down in her sitting room at Ibadan! We asked her to call neighbours to assist, so the corpse could be evacuated to the hospital. Instead of seeing this problem as my in-law's problem and asking my wife to call her siblings to handle the issue, I threw myself into the matter to the best of my abilities. I called the agent, who later mentioned that the lady had a chronic disease which he did not know, but he wanted to help the lady make some money as a result of poverty and pressure to visit Lagos, Nigeria. The greatest challenge we had was how to get the corpse to Cotonou through Idiroko border in Nigeria. On contacting friends at Ibadan, we got the death certificate and an ambulance from Adeoyo Hospital. The driver of the ambulance called "Alleluia" was very vibrant on phone when I spoke to him, assuring me that he knew the route through Ado-Awaye to Idiroko, which was the border town in Nigeria before Benin Republic. I also agreed with the agent to send some of the lady's relatives in Cotonou to come to the border, while sending some other relatives from Lagos. The plan was sealed. By 2pm that fateful day, the ambulance had arrived the border, awaiting our contacts from Lagos, meanwhile the police were already harassing the driver. Out of anger, the driver called his union members in Ibadan telling them to go seize my mother-in-law as he was being embarrassed, thinking that we did not make appropriate arrangements to receive the corpse. Meanwhile, the relatives of the deceased from the Lagos end were scared that the police will detain them and collect money from them. Even though we had given enough cash, they did not want to part with it. Eventually, they showed up, the police accosted them and made them write statements, collected and sighted the death certificate. The good thing the police did was that they supervised the handing over of the deceased to the family members who came in from Cotonou and released the 'Lagos contingent" as well as the ambulance driver, "Alleluia". On his release, he called me and mentioned that his colleagues at Ibadan had been recalled and asked to stay action. It was another challenge in my marital life. I had learnt my lesson, as these house help agents work in cahoots. They are a cartel. My family stopped patronizing them. Some of my sisters still do, but they ensure they go through necessary tests and are certified before they are engaged.

Health issues usually posed challenges for couples in

marriages. Some situations may just come one off or a flash in the pan, while some linger for months and years before they are overcome. These situations require a great deal of understanding, deep and regular communication and perseverance. A case that lends credence to this was a couple whose five year old son had malaria and was an outpatient in the wife's office clinic for about a week. The temperature, dizziness and weakness on the part of the boy did not abate at the end of seven days. The couple discussed and agreed that the boy should be taken to a family doctor, known over the years to the family as a great practitioner. The doctor gave the boy an injection, which made him sleep for about two hours, but unfortunately on waking up, the boy could not move the right side on which the injection was given. The parents were disturbed, though the doctor assured them that the boy was going to improve and get over the incident in a few days. Days ran into weeks; the wife started nagging and accusing the husband of engaging a quack doctor to treat their son! The husband endured all the annoyance and anger from the wife. He engaged a physiotherapist, as the boy was made to use crutches, so as to move around the house and in school. The physiotherapist visited regularly as scheduled for a year with little improvements on the movement of the boy's leg. Eventually, the wife being impatient, asked the physiotherapist to stop visiting, as she was going to continue with the child's exercises. On asking why she took that decision, she told the husband that a great amount was being expended on the exercises without any results, and that the husband should channel the savings to other things in the family! The husband was livid, thinking of his relationship with his medical professional, but he decided to stay calm. As the physiotherapist also recommended some drugs, surprisingly after about eighteen months the boy started walking freely with the two legs. Apart from a joyous reconciliation between husband and wife, the husband apologized to his medical professional.

ANNIVERSARIES

"Life is good only when it is magical and musical, a perfect timing and consent, and when we do not anatomize it."

Ralph Waldo Emerson

Obviously, anniversaries are moments of joy that we cherish, most especially when we celebrate with the one we love. Couples celebrate their birthdays, work anniversaries, wedding anniversaries, children's birthdays, the remembrance of a deceased loved one and old school events. All these make families and couples bond in marriage. The moment celebration of anniversaries cease in a family, things become stale. Not only when you pop champagne do you celebrate; but coming together, sharing of prayer, some popcorn and few drinks to remember the event goes a long way. People will view your family as a united and vibrant one.

Wasteful spending has been curbed with the experience of restrictions during COVID, even though couples want to have a big bash, they have realized unique ways of coming together to celebrate anniversaries and joyful moments by curtailing their spending. Some events where you would have had a buffet, nowadays you pack food of one or two choices. In remembrance of loved ones, some people now go straight to the vault, pray and give out packed lunch and drinks and everyone disperses. Back in the days, although some still do so, a special church service will be held and, from there, people retire home or to an event centre to wine and dine.

Some couples will not like to celebrate their wedding anniversaries, but they are usually taken aback when well wishers keep greeting them. Of course, they have forgotten that Facebook, LinkedIn, Twitter and all the social media they belong to will pick this up. When an event is in the social media, there is no longer any hiding place!

Celebrating my twenty-fifth wedding anniversary on the

social media in 2020, I received a great deal of teasing about my navy blue, "old school lapel" double breasted jacket on top of grey baggy trousers and my "polka dot" bow-tie on a half collar white shirt!! Someone said: "You can only wear this to a circus nowadays my brother!" And we had a good laugh!!

ENVISAGE THE STAGES
"The unexamined life is not worth living."

Socrates

"The mass of men lead lives of quiet desperation."

Henry Thoreau

In a conjugal arrangement, and to secure eternal bliss, it is necessary for couples to envisage the future and plan together, as they move from one stage of the marriage to another. It is high time you came to terms with your future!

The moment your children proceed to secondary school and move to the boarding house, you have to realize that they are leaving home gradually. They will pick up certain traits and idiosyncracies and make new friends. This will affect their relations with their siblings and also with you as parents. When they come home on holidays, you find out that the children may be better organized, waking up at a particular time, helping out on house chores and being very responsible. These are some behaviours picked up from the regimental life of the boarding house, which will assist their future life. You have to be more relaxed with the children as they now have a retinue of friends and acquaintances around your environment. So you should not be jittery when you have male friends coming to visit your female children. What you should emphasize is to guide their discussion, ensure they stay indoors and do not stay out late. When you over hear their discussions over the phone, and it does not align with contemporary living, you correct with love.

Another thing you need to address is to know the parents or the background of your children's friends. So when they inform you of their interest to attend parties with these friends, you envisage the relationship they can have, knowing the parents, where they live and what they do for a living. Meanwhile, by the time the children get to the higher institution, they tend to form greater opinions of their own and take a number of decisions without recourse to you as parents!! This is informed by their peers, the types of books they read, and what they are taught in the university. I remember one of my friends visiting me with his mum's car every weekend and coaching me on how to drive. This he did faithfully without informing his parents. They allowed him to drive their car, but not to the extent of turning himself to a driving school tutor! On the other hand, one of my brothers bashed our dad's car several times on the streets of Lagos. While he was able to settle some cases amicably with the car owners, he had to come home with some to discuss costs and terms of repairs! Eventually, he taught me how to drive. So you should be on guard to accept some of these situations of life and grow into them, not letting them get the better of you in annoyance or frustration.

You should put your mind at rest and pray a great deal as the children go into the National Service Year, where they have to travel across the country with different modes of transportation. This ranges from the plane to canoe through creeks in riverine areas. The children see this as an expedition and from there, they develop the zeal to succeed in life, breaking down any or every barrier to achieving their goals. Nowadays, parents are too anxious and keep fighting for the redeployment of their children from their place of primary assignment to their place of abode, hiding under security challenges. Meanwhile, some of these children will like to leave home at least for once and live independent lives. One of my friend's daughters refused to redeploy to Lagos despite her parents securing a transfer from Kano. She stayed the full nine months and eventually got a job in an accounting firm, where she is still practicing till date.

One of the challenges bedeviling elderly married couples now is the need for wives (grandmothers) to visit their children for a period to take care of newly-born children. The husband should have it in mind that a time will come when you will have to release your wife for one or two months for this exercise. The Igbos call it "Omugwo". While some husbands take it as one of the "rites of passage" and are ready to release their wives for the sake of their children and for proper nurturing of the newborn baby, some husbands frown at this, especially when the wife is staying more than necessary or going for a second visit. Some husbands threaten that they may likely get an acquaintance before their wives return! Since the birth of a child is a thing of joy, I feel families should make adequate preparations so that everything brings the desired joy all through.

Unity should be encouraged among siblings throughout their lifetimes! No matter their area of endeavour, couples should settle all grievances that arise amicably. As the adage goes: "You can not dislike your child to the extent that you will release it to a hungry lion." So grudges should be kept at the minimum and all issues arising from family squabbles must be discussed and settled accordingly. The mantra should be "you need each other" or "hold yourself together as the broom."

No matter how highly-placed or endowed couples are, they should reach out to their siblings and know what to do to assist when called upon. This lifts the pressure or strain off the extended family. We should not have "wealthy" versus "strugglers" within a family!

To encourage continuous communication and better relationship within the family, a particular father of a family who was a retired judge bequeathed one of his properties to all his children, apart from giving them individual properties. He believed that the particular property will bring them together from time to time for discussions, planning and relationships. This has manifested expeditiously as the children come together once in a while to discuss rent reviews, property renovation and remodeling, among others.

Couples should envisage mid-life crisis which comes in various forms and they should brace up for this, facing it with the utmost determination to overcome whatever challenges, and to go through the whole hog and length of time it exists. This can come in form of a job loss by the husband; this is bound to affect the family income despite rising overheads and bills. The wife has to support in whichever way, to enable them sail through the crisis. We have to console ourselves that: "when there is life, there is hope," as the saying goes. The crisis can come in the form of the need to relocate abruptly as a result of economic reasons. What of illness of one of the spouse or a child's drug addiction? What we find at times is that some couples start to pass the buck or blame each other for the cause of the crisis. You should just have it in mind that you will definitely overcome! What you need is constant communication and reaching out to people that you feel can assist. Do not begrudge anyone that could not assist in your moment of crisis, they were not billed to do so by God. Their purpose in your life may be different.

As we mentioned earlier, it is high time you came to terms with your future. For sure, there will be loneliness creeping in when all the children leave home, thus the need to cherish your partner. Couples move into smaller apartments so that their running expenses is reduced. Also, so that they can keep each other company more often. I have to sit in the kitchen at times while my wife is preparing food, so as to keep her company and also to get engaged myself. As regards food, you need to come up with a workable and affordable nourishing food timetable. By this, you will be able to keep away from the doctors and maintain good health.

To avoid loneliness, you need to maintain your relationships in your church, clubs, community, old students associations and take up roles that you can effectively perform. Recently, I delivered a lecture to the Elders of Thought of Ifako Ijaiye Community Development Association, Lagos. The theme was: "The Role of Elders in Community Development." I was not surprised that the association had laudable projects and the elders were determined to complete these projects. Thus, they engaged themselves, as well as community members from time to time. Such elders will not be lonely. It is pertinent to state that the Chairman of the Association, Chief Dapo Tawose, was my former boss while working at the Nigerian Bottling Company Ltd. Having retired over twenty-eight years ago, he still has the energy to lead a Community Development Association.

Having left home, your children will take it upon themselves to visit and check your welfare from time to time. Even when they are outside the shores of the country, they will still have the urge to see you physically – it is African! However, with their busy schedules which makes it difficult to see all your children at once, you will have to make do with modern technology to hold large family meetings. These include among others the MS Teams, Whatsapp, Zoom call, Goggle Meet and so on. This Information Technology advantage has solved a great deal of family crisis and fostered unity as envisaged.

Expect to get most information concerning your children through their mothers, and you should not make a fuss about it! Growing up, most of our requests were passed through our mums, so children will continue to sludge more to their mothers even after marriage! No surprise!

There have been some unexpected and unenvisaged descriptions to life that families had to cope with, such as the Covid-19 pandemic – we all weathered the storm. We commiserate with the families of those we lost during that period which affected the whole world! Meanwhile, a most recent crisis: a self-inflicted one at that, is the Monetary Policy introduced by the Central Bank of Nigeria late in 2022, with the resultant effect of its poor implementation, disrupting lives and businesses in the first quarter of 2023! We are still grappling with this crisis; thank God for the Supreme Court judgment that reversed the deadline of the Naira swap from 10 April 2023 to 31 December 2023. All hail the non-compromising Justices of the Supreme Court. I Peter 5:10 tells us: "But the God of all grace who hath called us into eternal glory by Christ Jesus, after that ye have suffered a while make you perfect, establish, strengthen, settle you."

WE HAVE TRUDGED THIS PATH BEFORE

"All these and lots more, we need to pass on to the next generation, who will then pass it on to the next generation, so they may arise and declare it to their children, so that they will get their hope in God and not forget the works of God." Psalm 78:3-7(paraphrased)

Yes, we come across them at the malls, the banks, the Church, at schools, at occasions, on the streets, in traffic and other places of interest – who? The next Generation!!! You try to correct them, they cannot hear you, because they have their earpiece permanently stuck in their ears! Those who hear do not pay attention, as they focus on their handsets for more interesting things, than what you intend to say to them. "That's why the street sweepers have been employed," shouted one young man who was challenged by an elderly man for throwing out thrash and empty cans out of his car while in traffic!

Talking of dressing, while the fashion of sagging is fading out gradually among the young men, the ladies do not see anything bad in showing off their cleavages, as some mothers do. So, who will correct who? Someone exclaimed the other day at an occasion: "Bobby no be private part again?" That is, the female breast should be taken as a comely part of the body and should be protected accordingly.

In traffic, the loud music, the astriding of lanes and the zig-zag movement between vehicles on top speed make you wonder if parents have actually done enough in moulding this next generation. Couples should insist on the continuous discipline of their children throughout their lifetime. In as much as you have to relax some rules, you have to continuously engage your children, so that they do not represent your family negatively. In our days, what elders ask is: "Omo ta niyen," meaning, "whose child is that?" This immediately refers to your family. Early in my sixth decade, my nonagenarian father still corrects me and gives reasons why I should see things from his point of view.

My younger sister, on coming home for vacation while in the secondary school, Queens College, Lagos, was scolded by an elderly man at the Yaba Bus Stop, when she was found dragging her box which had no tyre on the bare floor. According to her, the man said: "If the box is too heavy for you, let me put it on your head. Stop dragging it on the floor, lest you spoil it!" Immediately, she adjusted and corrected herself by lifting the box up properly. Such a man may be snubbed nowadays, as he may be seen as an intruder! The upcoming generation should be correctable and they should take to correction, as those correcting them know the consequences of not being correctable in the future.

Couples should have friends and mentors across the social strata. While you have mentors in the work place, you should also have people you admire and look up to in the society that you see as mentors you can emulate. Is it their truthfulness, their piousness or their style of handling difficult issues? As the mentoring concept teaches, your mentor does not or may not know that you have him as your mentor! We conclude this part by quoting Toyin Benson in his T – Ben-Series 110 as follows:

> "What our Fathers told us"
> That which we were told,
> That which we have read,
> That which we have known,
> That which we have seen,
> That which we have touched,
> And that which we have experienced,
> Should be told to the generations to
> come.

Tell them about:
> God's faithfulness

God's Goodness
God's Mercies
God's Benevolence
God's Abundance
God's Grace
God's Care
God's Love
God's Unlimited Blessings
God's Well Deserved Praises.

FASHIONISTA: ADOLESCENT TILL FADE

"Iri ni si, ni iso ni l'ojo"

Yoruba Proverb

Meaning: You will be addressed (honoured) by the way you dress

Growing up as an adult, being financially independent of parents, a great deal of money was planned for buying dresses, wristwatches, shoes and all sorts of items of fashion. Starting out as a classroom teacher, and on collecting my salary back then in the mid-1980s, together with some of my colleagues, we would hit the shops in Akure to buy shirts, trouser materials and at least a novel to read for the coming month. We even learnt some fashion concepts such as "when you wear a check shirt, then you wear a plain coloured tie." "Colour blocking" was another concept learnt, that is, you can only wear a plain shirt on multi-coloured trousers, and snickers on jeans trousers not lace up shoes. All these informed our dressing, which took a toll on our pockets in sustaining the standard. We had friends whose belts always matched their shoes, as well as their wristwatch straps. We had shoes of "crocodile skins" and "COBRA SKIN", shirts of various brands from Texen to Tommy Hilfiger, to St. Laurent, Raph Polo, YSL, etc. Our shirts must match our trousers; a sky blue shirt over a navy blue pair of trousers was very fashionable. "Colour riot" was the nickname given to friends who wore loud colours and who do not consider the uniqueness of their outfit.

As everyone began to go into marriage, very little emphasis was laid on continuously buying dresses, but we still remained fashionable, making sure our dresses complement that of our spouses. When a husband puts on teal green, the wife should put on a shade of green. The wife rather than friends should serve as the mirror for the husband, checking for fitness of dresses and correcting with love. While on outing, the wife should continuously see that the husband's dress is not soiled by avoiding rough and dirty paths.

As regards "Aso-ebi" (solicited and unsolicited uniforms) for social events, couples have to limit themselves to only necessary family events. The finances of the family will be negatively impacted if you continue to participate in every "Aso-Ebi" purchase presented to you. To avoid friction among couples, you need to discuss and agree if and when you are participating in the uniform concepts. Some couples feel shy because they feel they will look different or be the odd one out. I always suggest that you follow your conscience. When you buy Aso-ebi to satisfy your friends, but unable to meet your children's school or health needs, then you will have yourself to blame! Apparently, the husband that drops the funds just gets a strap of the dress to sew as cap, while the ladies adorn a major quantity of the dress. So you realize a "closed door meeting" is always necessary among couples before you dabble into such purchases – treat every occasion on its merits and circumstances at hand!!

ESSENTIAL MARITAL GLOSSARY

This section contains some essential words (though not exhaustive) that should be respected as they serve as oil to the machine of marital bliss. Apart from taking the meaning of the words literarily, couples should examine themselves and see how these words manifest in their marital life through their appropriate application.

A. Abundance: To have more than you need

   Affection: A gentle feeling of liking

B. Bond: A relationship between people based on shared feelings, interest and experiences

C. Companion: A person with whom you spend a great deal of time with.

   Courage: The ability to do something that frightens (bravery); mental or moral strength to venture, persevere and withstand danger, fear or difficulty.

D. Delight: Please someone tremendously

   Discernment: The ability to judge well; the quality of being able to grasp and comprehend what is obscure.

E. Endurance: The ability to tolerate an unpleasant or difficult process or situation without giving up.

F. Family: All descendants of a common ancestor; a group of one or more parents and their children living together as a unit.

   Favour: An act of kindness beyond what is due or usual. A liking for someone.

   Forgiveness: A conscious, deliberate decision to release feelings of resentment or vengeance toward a person or group who has harmed you,

		regardless of whether they actually deserve your forgiveness.
	Friendship:	A state of mutual trust and support between friends
G	Gentleness:	The quality of being mild, tender or mild-mannered.
	Gift:	A thing given willingly to a loved one without payment.
	Grace:	The free and unmerited favour of God, as manifested in the salvation of sinners and the bestowal of blessings (Christian belief); an attractively polite manner of behaving.
H.	Honesty:	Speaking and acting truthfully; showing respect towards others and having integrity and self awareness.
	Humility:	Freedom from pride and arrogance, acknowledging that you are smart but not all knowing, or have power but not omnipotent
I	Intimacy:	Close familiarity or friendship, togetherness, understanding, rapport.
J	Joy:	A feeling of great pleasure and happiness
L	Libido:	Sexual desire; the energy of the sexual drive as a component of the life instinct (psycho analysis)
	Loneliness:	Feelings of depression because someone has no friends or company. Constant and unrelenting feelings of being alone, separated or divided from others and an inability to connect on a deeper level.
	Love:	Intense feeling of deep affection for someone.
O	Obedience:	Submission to another's authority
	Openness:	The quality of being receptive to new ideas, opinions, or arguments, open mindednes.

Lack of secrecy or concealment

P. Patience: The capacity to accept or tolerate delay, problems or suffering without becoming annoyed or anxious.

Perseverance: Persistent in doing something despite difficulty or delay in achieving success.

Power: The capacity or ability to direct or influence the behaviour of others or the course of events.

Prudence: The ability to govern and discipline oneself by the use of reason, skill and good judgment in the management of affairs.

R. Respect: A feeling of deep admiration for someone or something elicited by their abilities, qualities or achievements.

S. Simplicity: The quality or condition of being easy to understand, being plain.

Sincerity: Display of absence of deceit, pretence, or hypocrisy, being serious, kind and truthful.

Supportive: Ability to provide encouragement and emotional help.

T. Tolerance: Capacity to endure pain or hardship; indulgence for beliefs or practices differing from or conflicting with one's own.

Trust: Firm believe in the reliability, truth, or ability of someone. Place confidence in someone.

W Wisdom: The quality of having experience, knowledge and good judgment, being wise.

COUNSELLORS SPEAK

TIPS FOR MARITAL LONGEVITY
Modupe Ehirim
The Right Fit Marriage Academy

Marital longevity refers to the length of time that a couple remains married, or the length of time that a marriage lasts. It is a measure of the stability and durability of a marriage and is often used as an indicator of the overall success of a marriage. Factors that can influence marital longevity include the quality of the relationship, the level of commitment and dedication, the ability to communicate effectively, and the presence of stress and challenges in the relationship. Additionally, external factors such as social and cultural norms, economic conditions, and access to resources and support can also play a role in determining marital longevity.

Factors That Affect Marital Longevity

1. **Quality of the relationship**: This refers to the level of intimacy, trust, mutual respect, and positive interaction between partners. A strong, healthy relationship is often characterized by open and effective communication, shared interests and goals, and a willingness to work together to overcome challenges.

2. **Level of commitment and dedication**: Couples who are committed to their relationship, and who are willing to make sacrifices and work together to achieve their goals are more likely to have a long-lasting marriage.

3. **Effective communication skills**: Good communication is key to any healthy relationship, and the ability to effectively communicate with each other is critical to maintaining a stable and lasting marriage. This includes listening actively, expressing needs and feelings in a clear and non-judgmental

way, and being able to resolve conflicts in a constructive manner.

4. **Ability to manage stress and challenges**: All marriages face challenges and stressors, such as financial difficulties, health problems, or conflicts with family members. Couples who are able to manage these challenges together by seeking support, compromising, and problem-solving, are more likely to have a long-lasting marriage.

5. **Social and cultural norms**: Social and cultural norms such as societal expectations of gender roles can influence a couple's relationship. For example, cultural attitudes towards divorce and marriage may impact a couple's decision to stay together or to seek a separation. In some cultures, a strong emphasis on individualism may lead to a greater emphasis on personal happiness, while in other cultures, a strong emphasis on collectivism may lead to a greater focus on maintaining social harmony in the relationship.

6. **Economic conditions**: Financial stability is an important factor in the success of a marriage, and couples who are able to work together to manage their finances and achieve financial security are more likely to have a lasting relationship. Financial stress and insecurity can lead to increased levels of conflict and tension, and can put a strain on the relationship.

7. **Access to resources and support**: Couples who have access to resources and support, such as therapy or counseling, or a strong network of friends and family, are more likely to be able to navigate challenges and maintain a stable relationship.

8. **Individual personality traits and emotional regulation skills**: Personal factors such as emotional regulation skills and personality traits can also play a role in determining

marital longevity. For example, individuals who are able to effectively manage their emotions and who are proactive in seeking support when needed are more likely to have a stable and long-lasting relationship.

9. **Previous relationship experiences**: Past experiences, such as previous marriages or long-term relationships, can influence a couple's relationship and their ability to navigate challenges.

10. **Family background and dynamics**: Family background and dynamics such as childhood experiences, family relationships, and cultural beliefs and values can shape an individual's attitudes and expectations about relationships, and can impact the ability of a couple to form and maintain a strong, lasting relationship. For example, growing up in a family with a strong emphasis on intimacy and emotional closeness may lead to a greater emphasis on these elements in a marriage, while growing up in a family that was characterized by conflict and instability may lead to difficulties in maintaining a lasting marriage.

Tips for Marital Longevity

1. **Prioritize your relationship**: Make your relationship a top priority and set aside time to connect and communicate with your partner.

2. **Practice active listening**: When your partner speaks, listen to them without interrupting or thinking about what you're going to say next. This can help to build trust and improve communication.

3. **Show appreciation and gratitude**: Express gratitude and appreciation for your partner regularly. Acknowledge their contributions to the relationship and show them that you value them.

4. **Manage conflicts constructively**: Conflicts are inevitable in any relationship, but it's important to manage them in a constructive and respectful manner. Seek to understand your partner's perspective and work together to find a resolution.

5. **Foster intimacy and emotional connection**: Maintain a strong emotional connection with your partner by engaging in activities that strengthen intimacy, such as shared hobbies or date nights.

6. **Seek outside help if needed**: If you're facing challenges in your relationship, don't be afraid to seek outside help. Consider couples therapy or counseling to work through difficulties and improve your relationship.

7. **Practice forgiveness and compromise**: Forgiveness and compromise are important for maintaining a strong and healthy relationship. Be willing to forgive your partner for their mistakes and be open to compromise on issues that are important to both of you.

8. **Work as a team**: Work together as a team to tackle challenges and achieve common goals. Marriage will bring its own set of challenges and stressors, but couples who are able to work together to manage these difficulties are more likely to have lasting marriages. By supporting each other and working together, you can strengthen your relationship and increase the likelihood of a long-lasting marriage.

9. **Maintain individual interests and identity**: While it's important to prioritize your relationship, it's also important to maintain your own individual interests and identity. This can help to keep the relationship fresh and prevent boredom or burnout.

10. **Invest in your relationship**: Regularly invest time, effort and resources into your relationship to keep it strong and healthy. This may include taking trips together, participating

in couples' therapy, or engaging in other activities that strengthen your bond.

11. **Build a strong support network**: Surrounding yourself with supportive family and friends can provide you with a network of resources and support that can help you navigate challenges and maintain your relationship.

EFFECTIVE COMMUNICATION IN MARRIAGE: A BIBLICAL PERSPECTIVE

Ven (Dr.) Adeyemi Agbelusi
Pioneer Director, School of Post-Graduate Studies, St Francis College of Theology, Wusasa, Zaria, Kaduna State

Marriage is a beautiful union between two people who have decided to love, cherish and support each other through thick and thin. However, the success of any marriage depends largely on the quality of communication between the partners. Communication is a critical aspect of any relationship, but it is especially crucial in marriage. In this article, we will explore the importance of effective communication in marriage from a Christian perspective, and provide some practical tips on how to improve communication in your marriage.

The Importance of Effective Communication in Marriage

Effective communication is vital in any relationship, but it is especially critical in marriage. Communication is the foundation of every healthy relationship, and it enables couples to understand each other's thoughts, feelings and needs. When communication is poor, it can lead to misunderstandings, conflicts and a breakdown in the relationship. In fact, studies have shown that poor communication is one of the leading causes of divorce.

Communication is essential in building a strong, healthy and God-honouring marriage. The Bible has much to say about the importance of communication in marriage. For instance, in Ephesians 4:29, the Bible says: "Let no corrupting talk come out of your mouths, but only such as is good for building up, as fits the occasion, that it may give grace to those who hear." This verse emphasizes the importance of speaking words that are edifying and uplifting, and not words that tear down and destroy.

Another important verse about communication in marriage is Proverbs 15:1, which says: "A soft answer turns away wrath, but a harsh word stirs up anger." This verse teaches us that the way we speak to our spouse can either diffuse or escalate a conflict. When we respond with a soft answer, we are more likely to resolve conflicts peacefully and maintain a healthy relationship.

Tips for Improving Communication in Your Marriage

Improving communication in your marriage requires intentional effort and a willingness to learn and grow together. Here are some practical tips that can help you improve communication in your marriage.

1. **Pay Attention**: Paying attention means fully concentrating on what your spouse is saying and responding in a way that shows you understand and empathize with their feelings. This involves paying attention to both verbal and nonverbal cues.

2. **Speak honestly and respectfully**: Honesty is crucial in any relationship, but it must be accompanied by respect. Avoid using harsh language or speaking in a demeaning tone, even when you disagree with your spouse.

3. **Communicate regularly**: Regular communication helps to strengthen the bond between you and your spouse. Make time for each other regularly and use that time to discuss important issues or just to catch up on each other's day.

4. **Avoid criticism and blame**: Criticism and blame can be hurtful and damaging to a relationship. Instead of blaming your spouse for issues, focus on finding solutions together.

5. **Pray together**: Prayer is a powerful tool that can help to improve communication in your marriage. Pray together

regularly, asking God for guidance, wisdom and grace as you work together to build a strong and healthy marriage.

6. **Active Listening**: Effective communication requires active listening. Active listening involves not only hearing what your spouse is saying, but also trying to understand their point of view. When couples fail to actively listen, misunderstandings can easily arise. Proverbs 18:13 states: "If one gives an answer before he hears, it is his folly and shame." It is essential to listen to your spouse's concerns and feelings without interrupting or jumping to conclusions. Listening with an open heart and mind can lead to a deeper understanding and connection between spouses.

7. **Use "I" Statements**: When communicating, it's important to use "I" statements instead of "you" statements. "I" statements express how you feel, while "you" statements can come across as accusatory. For example, saying: "I feel hurt when you don't listen to me" is more effective than saying "You never listen to me." Using "I" statements can help prevent defensiveness and encourage a more productive conversation. Ephesians 4:29 states: "Let no corrupting talk come out of your mouths, but only such as is good for building up, as fits the occasion, that it may give grace to those who hear." Using "I" statements can help build up your spouse and encourage healthy communication.

8. **Respectful Communication**: Respectful communication is essential in any relationship, especially in marriage. When communicating, it's important to speak respectfully and avoid harsh or critical language. Colossians 4:6 states: "Let your speech always be gracious, seasoned with salt, so that you may know how you ought to answer each person." Being respectful and kind can help prevent hurt feelings and promote a healthy dialogue between spouses.

9. **Avoid Negative Body Language**: Body language can speak louder than words. Negative body language such as eye-rolling, crossed arms or looking away can send negative signals to your spouse. Negative body language can escalate conflict and prevent effective communication. On the other hand, positive body language such as making eye contact, nodding and leaning in can signal active listening and promote a healthy dialogue. Proverbs 16:24 states: "Gracious words are like a honeycomb, sweetness to the soul and health to the body." Positive body language can reinforce gracious words and promote a healthy relationship.

10. **Take Responsibility**: Taking responsibility for your words and actions is crucial in effective communication. If you hurt your spouse's feelings, apologize and take steps to make things right. Taking responsibility for your actions can help prevent misunderstandings and promote forgiveness. James 5:16 states: "Therefore, confess your sins to one another and pray for one another, that you may be healed. The prayer of a righteous person has great power as it is working." Taking responsibility and seeking forgiveness can lead to healing and promote a stronger marriage.

Conclusion

Effective communication is vital in any marriage. Communication is not just a means of conveying information, but a way of showing love and respect to your spouse. The Bible teaches us that the way we speak to our spouse has a profound impact on the health of your marriage.

Effective communication is essential in building a strong and healthy marriage. Active listening, using "I" statements, respectful communication, avoiding negative body language and taking responsibility are all essential components of effective communication. Biblical principles such as respect, forgiveness and kindness can help promote healthy communication and build stronger marriages.

By following the practical tips outlined in this article and relying on God's guidance, you can improve communication in your marriage and build a strong and healthy relationship that honours God. As it says in Proverbs 18:21: "Death and life are in the power of the tongue, and those who love it will eat its fruits." Choose well.

PATIENCE, A POTENT TOOL FOR BLISSFUL MARRIAGE
Pastor Johnson Oluwasuji
A Marriage Counsellor with RCCG

"Patience is bitter, but its fruit is sweet"

Jean-Jacques Rousseau

Patience is an important skill to have in your marriage toolbox. It is so crucial for the success of your marriage. Lack of patience is destructive, and easily leads to saying or doing regretful things. In the marriage setting, you need to be patient with yourself, your spouse, your children and your marriage. Patience is a virtue. It is necessary for a healthy, happy and fulfilling marriage.

Marriage is a union of two different individuals, who come together to among other things, procreate to bring to life other different individuals. Individual differences are the traits or other characteristics by which individuals may be distinguished from one another. Individuals differ in physical forms (height, weight, colour, complexion, strength, etc.), intelligence, achievement, interest, attitude, aptitude, learning habits, skill and motor abilities. These individuals occupy the same space as it were. A great dose of patience is essential for the relationship to thrive. Relationship builds with love and care, but grows with patience and understanding. With patience, you understand the virtue of true love.

Patience is the ability to tolerate or restrain yourself from reacting in anger and frustration. You need patience for you to listen effectively to each other and understand each other. Without patience, you will not be able to discuss about money, housework, sex, children, etc., and resolve conflicts without fighting. Let your mood be calm and positive when dealing with your spouse (and children), even when they hurt or make you angry unintentionally, or even when your marriage is not what you want it to be. Surely, you will feel terrible moments after belittling your spouse (or child) just because you were angry about something trivial they did, more so when you cannot take those angry words back. Patience enables you to think before you react.

In your marriage, patience is particularly needed in the situations and circumstances highlighted underneath:

- When your marriage is not where you wish it were.
- When your spouse starts to vent frustration from a stressful day.
- When you have difficulty communicating with your spouse about things like money, sex, housework, house keeping allowance, children, in-laws, etc.
- When your spouse is not paying attention or listening to you while you have a conversation.
- When your children are being disrespectful, creating a mess or when they fail to do their chores.

Patience shows your spouse that you value him or her, and value your relationship enough to see beyond his or her "faults". Patience helps in developing the crucial relationship skill of empathy, which is the ability to understand life from the perspective of another. Patience will help you avoid becoming irritated, defensive and saying hurtful things. Patient people tend to experience less depression and negative emotions, perhaps because they can cope better with upsetting or stressful situations.

Patience is a skill that can be learned and practised. It is a result of choosing to emphasize "thinking" over "feeling". Some practical steps to become more patient are highlighted underneath:

- Practice patience daily
- Listen more than you talk

- Limit technology and other distractions
- Identify your triggers (e.g., things that anger you)
- Choose your timing for conversations well
- Manage your expectations
- Take a break. Pause before you say anything, particularly whenever you realize that you are loosing your patience
- Be an example of patience to your spouse
- Pray for patience
- Think and speak positively about your marriage
- Be open to new ways of doing things. See from other people's perspectives
- Be understanding. Apologize first. Encourage your spouse
- Be super quick to forgive. Don't raise your voice. Laugh more
- Give love, but give space too.

Marriage takes work, commitment and love, but they also need respect to be truly happy and successful. A marriage based on love and respect doesn't just happen. Both spouses have to do their part. Patience is undoubtedly one of the potent tools that holds a marriage together.